PUFFIN BOOKS

POEMS
for Over 10-Year-Olds

I've thought of a poem.
I carry it carefully,
nervously, in my head,
like a saucer of milk;
in case I should spill some lines
before I can put it down.

This rich and highly entertaining anthology of poems old
and new has been especially compiled for readers of ten
years old and more. It is a remarkably varied collection in
which classic and contemporary poems are successfully
intermingled. Terrifying poems about ghosts and ghouls;
exciting poems about highwaymen and smugglers;
poems about mysterious islands, lonesome ladies, lovable
animals, naughty children; funny, sweet, silly and musi-
cal poems; long romantic poems and short punchy poems
. . . something for everyone.

Kit Wright, former Education Officer of the Poetry
Society, has written several highly acclaimed and very
popular books of poetry for children. He has now brought
these talents to his work as an anthologist, and this enjoy-
able collection includes poems by William Shakespeare,
Lewis Carroll, Rudyard Kipling, Charles Causley, Hilaire
Belloc, A.A. Milne, Ted Hughes, Roger McGough and
many others. This is his second anthology for children.
His first, *Poems for 9-year-olds and Under,* is also published
in Puffin. Both anthologies contain marvellous illustrations by the award-winning artist, Michael Foreman.

D0232306

POEMS
for Over 10-Year-Olds

CHOSEN BY KIT WRIGHT
ILLUSTRATED BY MICHAEL FOREMAN

PUFFIN BOOKS

Puffin Books, Penguin Books Ltd, Harmondsworth, Middlesex, England
Viking Penguin Inc., 40 West 23rd Street, New York, New York, 10010, U.S.A.
Penguin Books Australia Ltd, Ringwood, Victoria, Australia
Penguin Books Canada Ltd, 2801 John Street, Markham, Ontario, Canada L3R 1B4
Penguin Books (N.Z.) Ltd, 182–190 Wairau Road, Auckland 10, New Zealand

First published by Viking Kestrel 1984
Published in Puffin Books 1985

This selection copyright © Kit Wright, 1984
Illustrations copyright © Michael Foreman, 1984
Copyright information for individual
poems is given on pages 190-92 which
constitute an extension of this
copyright page.
All rights reserved

Made and printed in Great Britain by
Richard Clay (The Chaucer Press) Ltd,
Bungay, Suffolk
Typeset in Palatino

Except in the United States of America,
this book is sold subject to the condition
that it shall not, by way of trade or otherwise,
be lent, re-sold, hired out, or otherwise circulated
without the publisher's prior consent in any form of
binding or cover other than that in which it is
published and without a similar condition
including this condition being imposed
on the subsequent purchaser

Contents

THOSE BRILLIANT CREATURES

IF YOU WAKE AT MIDNIGHT

A BUNCH OF THE BOYS

LONESOME LADIES

BATTLE ORDER

RIDDLES AND PUNS AND RUM CONUNDRUMS

AWFUL WARNINGS

SONGS AND SILENCES

I'VE THOUGHT
OF A POEM

Shallow Poem

I've thought of a poem.
I carry it carefully,
nervously, in my head,
like a saucer of milk;
in case I should spill some lines
before I can put it down.

GERDA MAYER

The Poem

It is only a little twig
With a green bud at the end;
But if you plant it,
And water it,
And set it where the sun will be above it,
It will grow into a tall bush
With many flowers,
And leaves which thrust hither and thither
Sparkling.
From its roots will come freshness,
And beneath it the grass-blades
Will bend and recover themselves,
And clash one upon another
In the blowing wind.

But if you take my twig
And throw it into a closet
With mousetraps and blunted tools,
It will shrivel and waste.
And, some day,
When you open the door,
You will think it an old twisted nail,
And sweep it into the dust bin
With other rubbish.

AMY LOWELL

The Door

Go and open the door.
   Maybe outside there's
   a tree, or a wood,
   a garden,
   or a magic city.

Go and open the door.
   Maybe a dog's rummaging.
   Maybe you'll see a face,
or an eye,
or the picture
          of a picture.

Go and open the door.
   If there's a fog
   it will clear.

Go and open the door.
   Even if there's only
   the darkness ticking,
   even if there's only
   the hollow wind,
   even if
       nothing
          is there,
go and open the door.

At least
there'll be
a draught.

MIROSLAV HOLUB

trans. IAN MILNER and

GEORGE THEINER

WHEN I WAS YOUR AGE

When That I Was and a Little Tiny Boy

When that I was and a little tiny boy,
  With hey, ho, the wind and the rain;
A foolish thing was but a toy,
  For the rain it raineth every day.

But when I came to man's estate,
  With hey, ho, the wind and the rain:
'Gainst knaves and thieves men shut their gate,
  For the rain it raineth every day.

But when I came, alas, to wive,
  With hey, ho, the wind and the rain:
By swaggering could I never thrive,
  For the rain it raineth every day.

A great while ago the world was begun,
  With hey, ho, the wind and the rain,
But that's all one, our play is done,
  And we'll strive to please you every day.

WILLIAM SHAKESPEARE

When I Was Your Age

When I was your age, child –
When I was eight,
When I was ten,
When I was two
(How old are you?) –
When I was your age, child,
My father would have gone quite *wild*
Had I behaved the way you
Do.
What, food uneaten on my plate
When I was eight?
What, room in such a filthy state
When I was ten?
What, late
For school when I was two?
My father would have shouted, 'When
I was your age, child, my father would have *raved*
Had I behaved
The way you
Do.'

When I was
Your age, child, I did not drive us
All perpetually mad
By bashing
Up my little brother and reducing him to tears.
There was a war on in those years!
There were no brothers to be had!
Even sisters were on ration!

My goodness, we were pleased
To get *anything* to tease!
We were glad
Of aunts and dogs,
Of chickens, grandmothers, and frogs;
Of creatures finned and creatures hooved,
And second cousins twice removed!

When I was your
Age, child, I was more
Considerate of others
(Particularly of fathers and of mothers).
I did not sprawl
Reading the *Dandy*
Or the *Beano*
When aunts and uncles came to call.
Indeed no.
I grandly
Entertained them all
With 'Please' and 'Thank you,' 'May I . . .?'
　 'Thank you,' 'Sorry,' 'Please,'
And other remarks like these.
And if a chance came in the conversation
I would gracefully recite a line
Which everyone recognized as a quotation
From one of the higher multiplication
Tables, like 'Seven sevens are forty-nine.'

When I was your age, child, I
Should never have dreamed
Of sitting idly
Watching television half the night.

It would have seemed
Demented:
Television not then having been
Invented.

When I
Was your age, child, I did not lie
About
The house all day.
(I did not lie about anything at all – no liar I!)
I got out!
I ran away
To sea!
(Though naturally I was back, with hair brushed
    and hands washed, in time for tea.)
Oh yes, goodness me,
When I was nine
I had worked already down a diamond mine,
And fought in several minor wars,
And hunted boars

In the lonelier
Parts of Patagonia.
(Though I admit that possibly by then
I was getting on for ten.)
In the goldfields of Australia
I learned the bitterness of failure;
Experience in the temples of Siam
Made me the wise and punctual man I am;
But the lesson that I value most
I learned upon the Coromandel Coast –
Never, come what may, to boast.

When
I was your age, child, and the older generation
Offered now and then
A kindly explanation
Of what the world was like in their young day
I did not yawn in that rude way.
Why, goodness me,
There being no television to see
(As I have, I think, already said)
We were dashed grateful
For any entertainment we could get instead,
However tedious and hateful.

So grow up, child! And be
Your age! (What *is* your age, then?
Eight? Or nine? Or two? Or ten?)
Remember, as you look at me –
When I was your age I was forty-three.

MICHAEL FRAYN

The Lesson

A poem that raises the question:
Should there be capital punishment in schools?

Chaos ruled OK in the classroom
as bravely the teacher walked in
the nooligans ignored him
his voice was lost in the din

'The theme for today is violence
and homework will be set
I'm going to teach you a lesson
one that you'll never forget'

He picked on a boy who was shouting
and throttled him then and there
then garrotted the girl behind him
(the one with grotty hair)

Then sword in hand he hacked his way
between the chattering rows
'First come, first severed' he declared
'fingers, feet, or toes'

He threw the sword at a latecomer
it struck with deadly aim
then pulling out a shotgun
he continued with his game

The first blast cleared the backrow
(where those who skive hang out)
they collapsed like rubber dinghies
when the plug's pulled out

'Please may I leave the room sir?'
a trembling vandal enquired
'Of course you may' said teacher
put the gun to his temple and fired

The Head popped a head round the doorway
to see why a din was being made
nodded understandingly
then tossed in a grenade

And when the ammo was well spent
with blood on every chair
Silence shuffled forward
with its hands up in the air

The teacher surveyed the carnage
the dying and the dead
He waggled a finger severely
'Now let that be a lesson' he said

ROGER McGOUGH

Meet-on-the-Road

'Now, pray, where are you going?' said Meet-on-the-Road.
'To school, sir, to school, sir,' said Child-as-it-Stood.

'What have you in your basket, child?' said Meet-on-the-Road.
'My dinner, sir, my dinner, sir,' said Child-as-it-Stood.

'What have you for dinner, child?' said Meet-on-the-Road.
'Some pudding, sir, some pudding, sir,' said Child-as-it-Stood.

'Oh, then I pray, give me a share,' said Meet-on-the-Road.
'I've little enough for myself, sir,' said Child-as-it-Stood.

'What have you got that cloak on for?' said Meet-on-the-Road.
'To keep the wind and cold from me,' said Child-as-it-Stood.

'I wish the wind would blow through you,' said Meet-on-the-Road.
'Oh, what a wish! What a wish!' said Child-as-it-Stood.

'Pray, what are those bells ringing for?' said Meet-on-the-Road.
'To ring bad spirits home again,' said Child-as-it-Stood.

'Oh, then I must be going, child!' said Meet-on-the-Road.
'So fare you well, so fare you well,' said Child-as-it-Stood.

ANON.

Nursery Rhyme of Innocence and Experience

I had a silver penny
  And an apricot tree
And I said to the sailor
  On the white quay

'Sailor O sailor
  Will you bring me
If I give you my penny
  And my apricot tree

'A fez from Algeria
  An Arab drum to beat
A little gilt sword
  And a parakeet?'

And he smiled and he kissed me
  As strong as death
And I saw his red tongue
  And I felt his sweet breath

'You may keep your penny
  And your apricot tree
And I'll bring your presents
  Back from sea.'

O the ship dipped down
  On the rim of the sky
And I waited while three
  Long summers went by

Then one steel morning
  On the white quay
I saw a grey ship
  Come in from sea

Slowly she came
  Across the bay
For her flashing rigging
  Was shot away

All round her wake
  The seabirds cried
And flew in and out
  Of the hole in her side

Slowly she came
  In the path of the sun
And I heard the sound
  Of a distant gun

And a stranger came running
  Up to me
From the deck of the ship
  And he said, said he

'O are you the boy
  Who would wait on the quay
With the silver penny
  And the apricot tree?

'I've a plum-coloured fez
   And a drum for thee
And a sword and a parakeet
   From over the sea.'

'O where is the sailor
   With bold red hair?
And what is that volley
   On the bright air?

'O where are the other
   Girls and boys?
And why have you brought me
   Children's toys?'

CHARLES CAUSLEY

Old Father William

(from *Alice in Wonderland*)

'You are old, father William,' the young man said,
  'And your hair has become very white;
And yet you incessantly stand on your head –
  Do you think, at your age, it is right?'

'In my youth,' father William replied to his son,
  'I feared it might injure the brain;
But, now that I'm perfectly sure I have none,
  Why, I do it again and again.'

'You are old,' said the youth, 'as I mentioned before,
  And have grown most uncommonly fat;
Yet you turned a back-somersault in at the door –
  Pray what is the reason of that?'

'In my youth,' said the sage, as he shook his grey locks,
  'I kept all my limbs very supple
By the use of this ointment – one shilling the box –
  Allow me to sell you a couple?'

'You are old,' said the youth, 'and your jaws are too weak
  For anything tougher than suet;
Yet you finished the goose, with the bones and the beak –
  Pray, how did you manage to do it?'

'In my youth,' said his father, 'I took to the law,
  And argued each case with my wife;
And the muscular strength, which it gave to my jaw,
  Has lasted the rest of my life.'

'You are old,' said the youth, 'one would hardly suppose
   That your eye was as steady as ever;
Yet you balanced an eel on the end of your nose –
   What made you so awfully clever?'

'I have answered three questions, and that is enough,'
   Said his father. 'Don't give yourself airs!
Do you think I can listen all day to such stuff?
   Be off, or I'll kick you downstairs!'

LEWIS CARROLL

STOPPING BY WOODS

Stopping by Woods on a Snowy Evening

Whose woods these are I think I know.
His house is in the village though;
He will not see me stopping here
To watch his woods fill up with snow.

My little horse must think it queer
To stop without a farmhouse near
Between the woods and frozen lake
The darkest evening of the year.

He gives his harness bells a shake
To ask if there is some mistake.
The only other sound's the sweep
Of easy wind and downy flake.

The woods are lovely, dark and deep.
But I have promises to keep,
And miles to go before I sleep,
And miles to go before I sleep.

ROBERT FROST

Loveliest of Trees

(from *A Shropshire Lad*)

Loveliest of trees, the cherry now
Is hung with bloom along the bough,
And stands about the woodland ride
Wearing white for Eastertide.

Now, of my threescore years and ten,
Twenty will not come again,
And take from seventy springs a score,
It only leaves me fifty more.

And since to look at things in bloom
Fifty springs are little room,
About the woodlands I will go
To see the cherry hung with snow.

A. E. HOUSMAN

Weathers

I

This is the weather the cuckoo likes
    And so do I;
When showers betumble the chestnut spikes,
    And nestlings fly:
And the little brown nightingale bills his best,
And they sit outside at 'The Travellers' Rest',
And maids come forth sprig-muslin drest,
And citizens dream of the south and west
    And so do I.

II

This is the weather the shepherd shuns,
    And so do I;
When beeches drip in browns and duns,
    And thresh, and ply;
And hill-hid tides throb, throe on throe,
And meadow rivulets overflow,
And drops on gate-bars hang in a row,
And rooks in families homeward go,
    And so do I.

THOMAS HARDY

Meg Merrilees

Old Meg she was a gypsy,
    And lived upon the moors:
Her bed it was the brown heath turf,
    And her house was out of doors.

Her apples were swart blackberries,
    Her currants pods o' broom;
Her wine was dew of the wild white rose,
    Her book a churchyard tomb.

Her Brothers were the craggy hills,
    Her Sisters larchen trees;
Alone with her great family
    She lived as she did please.

No breakfast had she many a morn,
    No dinner many a noon,
And 'stead of supper she would stare
    Full hard against the moon.

But every morn of woodbine fresh
    She made her garlanding
And every night the dark glen Yew
    She wove, and she would sing.

And with her fingers, old and brown,
    She plaited Mats o' Rushes,
And gave them to the Cottagers
    She met among the Bushes.

Old Meg was brave as Margaret Queen,
    And tall as Amazon;
An old red blanket cloak she wore;
    A chip hat had she on.
God rest her aged bones somewhere –
    She died full long agone!

JOHN KEATS

Summer

Winter is cold-hearted,
   Spring is yea and nay,
Autumn is a weathercock
   Blown every way:
Summer days for me
When every leaf is on the tree;

When Robin's not a beggar,
   And Jenny Wren's a bride,
And larks hang singing, singing, singing,
    Over the wheatfields wide,
    And anchored lilies ride,
And the pendulum spider
   Swings from side to side,

And blue-black beetles transact business,
   And gnats fly in a host,
And furry caterpillars hasten
   That no time be lost,
And moths grow fat and thrive,
And ladybirds arrive.

Before green apples blush,
   Before green nuts embrown,
Why, one day in the country
   Is worth a month in town;
   Is worth a day and a year
Of the dusty, musty, lag-last fashion
   That days drone elsewhere.

CHRISTINA ROSSETTI

Tall Nettles

Tall nettles cover up, as they have done
These many springs, the rusty harrow, the plough
Long worn out, and the roller made of stone:
Only the elm butt tops the nettles now.

This corner of the farmyard I like most:
As well as any bloom upon a flower
I like the dust on the nettles, never lost
Except to prove the sweetness of a shower.

EDWARD THOMAS

Nettles

My son aged three fell in the nettle bed.
'Bed' seemed a curious name for those green spears,
That regiment of spite behind the shed:
It was no place for rest. With sobs and tears
The boy came seeking comfort and I saw
White blisters beaded on his tender skin.
We soothed him till his pain was not so raw.
At last he offered us a watery grin,
And then I took my hook and honed the blade
And went outside and slashed in fury with it
Till not a nettle in that fierce parade
Stood upright anymore. Next task: I lit
A funeral pyre to burn the fallen dead.
But in two weeks the busy sun and rain
Had called up tall recruits behind the shed:
My son would often feel sharp wounds again.

VERNON SCANNELL

The Way through the Woods

They shut the road through the woods
Seventy years ago.
Weather and rain have undone it again
And now you would never know
There was once a road through the woods
Before they planted the trees.
It is underneath the coppice and heath
And the thin anemones.
Only the keeper sees
That, where the ring-dove broods,
And the badgers roll at ease,
There was once a road through the woods.

Yet, if you enter the woods
Of a summer evening late,
When the night air cools on the trout-ringed pools
Where the otter whistles his mate,
(They fear not man in the woods
Because they see so few),
You will hear the beat of a horse's feet,
And the swish of a skirt in the dew,
Steadily cantering through
The misty solitudes,
As though they perfectly knew
The old lost road through the woods ...
But there is no road through the woods!

RUDYARD KIPLING

The Listeners

'Is there anybody there?' said the Traveller,
  Knocking on the moonlit door;
And his horse in the silence champed the grasses
  Of the forest's ferny floor:
And a bird flew up out of the turret,
  Above the Traveller's head:
And he smote upon the door a second time;
  'Is there anybody there?' he said.
But no one descended to the Traveller;
  No head from the leaf-fringed sill
Leaned over and looked into his grey eyes,
  Where he stood perplexed and still.
But only a host of phantom listeners
  That dwelt in the lone house then
Stood listening in the quiet of the moonlight
  To that voice from the world of men:
Stood thronging the faint moonbeams on the dark stair,
  That goes down to the empty hall,
Hearkening in an air stirred and shaken
  By the lonely Traveller's call.
And he felt in his heart their strangeness,
  Their stillness answering his cry,
While his horse moved, cropping the dark turf,
  'Neath the starred and leafy sky;
For he suddenly smote on the door, even
  Louder, and lifted his head:
'Tell them I came, and no one answered,
  That I kept my word,' he said.

Never the least stir made the listeners,
  Though every word he spake
Fell echoing through the shadowiness of the still house
  From the one man left awake:
Ay, they heard his foot upon the stirrup,
  And the sound of iron on stone,
And how the silence surged softly backward,
  When the plunging hoofs were gone.

WALTER DE LA MARE

THOSE BRILLIANT
CREATURES

The Lamb

Little Lamb, who made thee?
  Dost thou know who made thee?
Gave thee life and bid thee feed,
By the stream, and o'er the mead;
Gave thee clothing of delight,
Softest clothing, woolly, bright;
Gave thee such a tender voice,
Making all the vales rejoice?
  Little Lamb, who made thee?
  Dost thou know who made thee?

Little Lamb, I'll tell thee,
  Little Lamb, I'll tell thee:
He is called by thy name,
For he calls himself a Lamb.
He is meek, and he is mild;
He became a little child.
I a child, and thou a lamb.
We are called by his name.
  Little Lamb, God bless thee!
  Little Lamb, God bless thee!

WILLIAM BLAKE

The Wild Swans at Coole

The trees are in their autumn beauty,
The woodland paths are dry,
Under the October twilight the water
Mirrors a still sky;
Upon the brimming water among the stones
Are nine-and-fifty swans.

The nineteenth autumn has come upon me
Since I first made my count;
I saw, before I had well finished,
All suddenly mount
And scatter wheeling in great broken rings
Upon their clamorous wings.

I have looked upon those brilliant creatures,
And now my heart is sore.
All's changed since I, hearing at twilight,
The first time on this shore,
The bell-beat of their wings above my head,
Trod with a lighter tread.

Unwearied still, lover by lover,
They paddle in the cold
Companionable streams or climb the air;
Their hearts have not grown old;
Passion or conquest, wander where they will,
Attend upon them still.

But now they drift on the still water,
Mysterious, beautiful;
Among what waters will they build,
By what lake's edge or pool
Delight men's eyes when I awake some day
To find they have flown away?

W. B. YEATS

The Eagle

He clasps the crag with crooked hands;
Close to the sun in lonely lands,
Ring'd with the azure world, he stands,

The wrinkled sea beneath him crawls;
He watches from his mountain walls,
And like a thunderbolt he falls.

ALFRED, LORD TENNYSON

The Tyger

Tyger! Tyger! burning bright
In the forests of the night,
What immortal hand or eye
Could frame thy fearful symmetry?

In what distant deeps or skies
Burnt the fire of thine eyes?
On what wings dare he aspire?
What the hand dare seize the fire?

And what shoulder, and what art,
Could twist the sinews of thy heart?
And when thy heart began to beat,
What dread hand? And what dread feet?

What the hammer? what the chain?
In what furnace was thy brain?
What the anvil? what dread grasp
Dare its deadly terrors clasp?

When the stars threw down their spears,
And water'd heaven with their tears,
Did he smile his work to see?
Did he who made the Lamb make thee?

Tyger! Tyger! burning bright
In the forests of the night,
What immortal hand or eye
Dare frame thy fearful symmetry?

WILLIAM BLAKE

When Cats Run Home

When cats run home and light is come,
    And dew is cold upon the ground,
And the far-off stream is dumb,
    And the whirring sail goes round,
    And the whirring sail goes round;
      Alone and warming his five wits,
      The white owl in the belfry sits.

When merry milkmaids click the latch,
    And rarely smells the new-mown hay,
And the cock hath sung beneath the thatch
    Twice or thrice his roundelay,
    Twice or thrice his roundelay;
      Alone and warming his five wits,
      The white owl in the belfry sits.

ALFRED, LORD TENNYSON

The Flower-fed Buffaloes

The flower-fed buffaloes of the spring
In the days of long ago,
Ranged where the locomotives sing
And the prairie flowers lie low:
The tossing, blooming, perfumed grass
Is swept away by the wheat,
Wheels and wheels and wheels spin by
In the spring that still is sweet.
But the flower-fed buffaloes of the spring
Left us, long ago.
They gore no more, they bellow no more,
They trundle around the hills no more:
With the Blackfeet, lying low,
With the Pawnees, lying low,
Lying low.

VACHEL LINDSAY

The Lost Heifer

When the black herds of the rain were grazing
In the gap of the pure cold wind
And the watery haze of the hazel
Brought her into my mind,
I thought of the last honey by the water
That no hive can find.

Brightness was drenching through the branches
When she wandered again,
Turning the silver out of dark grasses
Where the skylark had lain,
And her voice coming softly over the meadow
Was the mist becoming rain.

AUSTIN CLARKE

Sheep

When I was once in Baltimore,
   A man came up to me and cried,
'Come, I have eighteen hundred sheep,
   And we sail on Tuesday's tide.

'If you will sail with me, young man,
   I'll pay you fifty shillings down;
These eighteen hundred sheep I take
   From Baltimore to Glasgow town.'

He paid me fifty shillings down,
   I sailed with eighteen hundred sheep;
We soon had cleared the harbour's mouth,
   We soon were in the salt sea deep.

The first night we were out at sea
   Those sheep were quiet in their mind;
The second night they cried with fear –
   They smelt no pastures in the wind.

They sniffed, poor things, for their green fields,
   They cried so loud I could not sleep:
For fifty thousand shillings down
   I would not sail again with sheep.

W. H. DAVIES

From *Reynard the Fox*

The fox was strong, he was full of running,
He could run for an hour and then be cunning,
But the cry behind him made him chill,
They were nearer now and they meant to kill.
They meant to run him until his blood
Clogged on his heart as his brush with mud,
Till his back bent up and his tongue hung flagging
And his belly and brush were filthed from dragging,
Till he crouched stone-still, dead-beat and dirty,
With nothing but teeth against the thirty.
And all the way to that blinding end
He would meet with men and have none his friend:
Men to holloa and men to run him,
With stones to stagger and yells to stun him;
Men to head him, with whips to beat him;
Teeth to mangle and mouths to eat him.
And all the way, that wild high crying,
To cold his blood with the thought of dying,
The horn and the cheer, and the drum-like thunder
Of the horse-hooves stamping the meadows under.
He upped his brush and went with a will
For the Sarsen Stones on Wan Dyke Hill.

JOHN MASEFIELD

From *A Runnable Stag*

When the pods went pop on the broom, green broom,
  And apples began to be golden-skinned,
We harboured a stag by the Priory coomb,
  And we feathered his trail up-wind, up-wind,
  We feathered his trail up-wind –
    A stag of warrant, a stag, a stag,
    A runnable stag, a kingly crop,
    Brown, bay and tray and three on top,
    A stag, a runnable stag . . .

For a matter of twenty miles and more,
  By the densest hedge and the highest wall,
Through herds of bullocks he baffled the lore
  Of harbourer, huntsman, hounds and all,
  Of harbourer, hounds and all –
    The stag of warrant, the wily stag,
    For twenty miles, and five and five,
    He ran, and he never was caught alive,
    This stag, this runnable stag . . .

Three hundred gentlemen, able to ride,
  Three hundred horses as gallant and free,
Beheld him escape on the evening tide,
  Far out till he sank in the Severn Sea,
  Till he sank in the depths of the sea –
    The stag, the buoyant stag, the stag
    That slept at last in a jewelled bed
    Under the sheltering ocean spread,
    The stag, the runnable stag.

JOHN DAVIDSON

How Doth the Little Crocodile

(from *Alice in Wonderland*)

How doth the little crocodile
   Improve his shining tail,
And pour the waters of the Nile
   On every golden scale!

How cheerfully he seems to grin,
   How neatly spreads his claws,
And welcomes little fishes in,
   With gently smiling jaws!

LEWIS CARROLL

Worm Sonnet

Ah wonderful the wriggle of the worm
   Who wiggle-wags his woozy way in tunnels:
So sensitive to sunshine he must squirm
   Through midnight slime in sloshy little runnels;

Then, when it rains, his caverns fill with slurry
   To drive him up his labyrinthine funnels
Through many a shaft and adit — he must hurry:
   His miry mine gets flooded to the gun'ls.

When the storm is over, down he'll flop
   To clean the floods out of his loo and larder:
Deprived of hoover, Xpelair or mop
   His lot (compared with housewives') is much harder.

Without steambaths and piemash in the diner,
A worm is even worse off than a miner.

MICHAEL BALDWIN

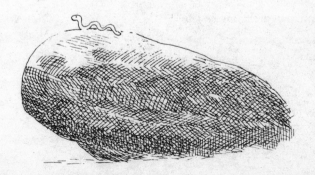

Bat

At evening, sitting on this terrace,
When the sun from the west, beyond Pisa, beyond the mountains of
    Carrara
Departs, and the world is taken by surprise ...

When the tired flower of Florence is in gloom beneath the glowing
Brown hills surrounding ...

When under the arches of the Ponte Vecchio
A green light enters against stream, flush from the west,
Against the current of obscure Arno ...

Look up, and you see things flying
Between the day and the night;
Swallows with spools of dark thread sewing the shadows together.

A circle swoop, and a quick parabola under the bridge arches
Where light pushes through;
A sudden turning upon itself of a thing in the air,
A dip to the water.

And you think:
'The swallows are flying so late!'

Swallows?

Dark air-life looping
Yet missing the pure loop ...

A twitch, a twitter, an elastic shudder in flight
And serrated wings against the sky,
Like a glove, a black glove thrown up at the light,
And falling back.

Never swallows!
Bats!
The swallows are gone.

At a wavering instant the swallows gave way to bats
By the Ponte Vecchio ...
Changing guard.

Bats, and an uneasy creeping in one's scalp
As the bats swoop overhead!
Flying madly.

Pipistrello!
Black piper on an infinitesimal pipe.
Little lumps that fly in air and have voices indefinite, wildly vindictive;

Wings like bits of umbrella.

Bats!

Creatures that hang themselves up like an old rag, to sleep;
And disgustingly upside down.

Hanging upside down like rows of disgusting old rags
And grinning in their sleep.
Bats!

Not for me!

D. H. LAWRENCE

After Prévert

We are going to see the rabbit,
We are going to see the rabbit.
Which rabbit, people say?
Which rabbit, ask the children?
Which rabbit?
The only rabbit,
The only rabbit in England,
Sitting behind a barbed-wire fence
Under the floodlights, neon lights,
Sodium lights,
Nibbling grass
On the only patch of grass
In England, in England
(Except the grass by the hoardings
Which doesn't count.)
We are going to see the rabbit
And we must be there on time.

First we shall go by escalator,
Then we shall go by underground,
And then we shall go by motorway
And then by helicopterway
And the last ten yards we shall have to go
On foot.

And now we are going
All the way to see the rabbit,
We are nearly there,
We are longing to see it,

And so is the crowd
Which is here in thousands
With mounted policemen
And big loudspeakers
And bands and banners,
And everyone has come a long way.
But soon we shall see it
Sitting and nibbling
The blades of grass
On the only patch of grass
In — but something has gone wrong!
Why is everyone so angry,
Why is everyone jostling
And slanging and complaining?

The rabbit has gone,
Yes, the rabbit has gone.
He has actually burrowed down into the earth
And made himself a warren, under the earth,
Despite all these people,
And what shall we do?
What *can* we do?

It is all a pity, you must be disappointed,
Go home and do something else for today,
Go home again, go home for today.
For you cannot hear the rabbit under the earth,
Remarking rather sadly to himself, by himself,
As he rests in his warren under the earth:
'It won't be long, they are bound to come,
They are bound to come and find me, even here.'

ALAN BROWNJOHN

The Camel's Hump

The camel's hump is an ugly lump
  Which well you may see at the Zoo;
But uglier yet is the hump we get
  From having too little to do.

Kiddies and grown-ups too-oo-oo,
If we haven't enough to doo-oo-oo,
        We get the hump –
        Cameelious hump –
The hump that is black and blue!

We climb out of bed with a frouzly head,
  And a snarly-yarly voice.
We shiver and scowl and we grunt and we growl
  At our bath and our boots and our toys!

And there ought to be a corner for me
(And I know there is one for you)
        When we get the hump –
        Cameelious hump –
The hump that is black and blue!

The cure for this ill is not to sit still,
  Or frowst with a book by the fire;
But to take a large hoe and a shovel also,
  And dig till you gently perspire;

And then you will find that the sun and the wind,
And the Djinn of the Garden too,
      Have lifted the hump –
      The horrible hump –
The hump that is black and blue!

I get it as well as you-oo-oou,
If I haven't enough to do-oo-oo!
      We all get the hump –
      Cameelious hump –
Kiddies and grown-ups too!

RUDYARD KIPLING

Hunter Trials

It's awf'lly bad luck on Diana,
    Her ponies have swallowed their bits;
She fished down their throats with a spanner
    And frightened them all into fits.

So now she's attempting to borrow.
    Do lend her some bits, Mummy, *do*;
I'll lend her my own for tomorrow,
    But today I'll be wanting them too.

Just look at Prunella on Guzzle,
    The wizardest pony on earth;
Why doesn't she slacken his muzzle
    And tighten the breech in his girth?

I say, Mummy, there's Mrs Geyser
    And doesn't she look pretty sick?
I bet it's because Mona Lisa
    Was hit on the hock with a brick.

Miss Blewitt says Monica threw it,
    But Monica says it was Joan,
And Joan's very thick with Miss Blewitt,
    So Monica's sulking alone.

And Margaret failed in her paces,
    Her withers got tied in a noose,
So her coronet's caught in the traces
    And now all her fetlocks are loose.

Oh, it's me now. I'm terribly nervous.
    I wonder if Smudges will shy.
She's practically certain to swerve as
    Her Pelham is over one eye.

*   *   *

Oh, wasn't it naughty of Smudges?
    Oh, Mummy, I'm sick with disgust.
She threw me in front of the Judges,
    And my silly old collarbone's bust.

JOHN BETJEMAN

The Lobster Quadrille

(from *Alice in Wonderland*)

'Will you walk a little faster?' said a whiting to a snail,
'There's a porpoise close behind us, and he's treading on my tail.
See how eagerly the lobsters and the turtles all advance!
They are waiting on the shingle — will you come and join the dance?
  Will you, won't you, will you, won't you, will you join the dance?
  Will you, won't you, will you, won't you, won't you join the dance?

'You can really have no notion how delightful it will be
When they take us up and throw us, with the lobsters, out to sea!'
But the snail replied 'Too far, too far!' and gave a look askance —
Said he thanked the whiting kindly, but he would not join the dance.
  Would not, could not, would not, could not, would not join the
    dance.
  Would not, could not, would not, could not, could not join the
    dance.

'What matters it how far we go?' his scaly friend replied.
'There is another shore, you know, upon the other side.
The further off from England the nearer is to France —
Then turn not pale, beloved snail, but come and join the dance.
  Will you, won't you, will you, won't you, will you join the dance?
  Will you, won't you, will you, won't you, won't you join the dance?'

LEWIS CARROLL

The Walrus and the Carpenter

(from *Through the Looking-Glass*)

The sun was shining on the sea,
　　Shining with all his might:
He did his very best to make
　　The billows smooth and bright –
And this was odd, because it was
　　The middle of the night.

The moon was shining sulkily,
　　Because she thought the sun
Had got no business to be there
　　After the day was done –
'It's very rude of him,' she said,
　　'To come and spoil the fun!'

The sea was wet as wet could be,
　　The sands were dry as dry.
You could not see a cloud because
　　No cloud was in the sky:
No birds were flying overhead –
　　There were no birds to fly.

The Walrus and the Carpenter
　　Were walking close at hand:
They wept like anything to see
　　Such quantities of sand:
'If this were only cleared away,'
　　They said, 'it would be grand!'

'If seven maids with seven mops
　　Swept it for half a year,
Do you suppose,' the Walrus said,
　　'That they could get it clear?'
'I doubt it,' said the Carpenter,
　　And shed a bitter tear.

'O Oysters, come and walk with us!'
　　The Walrus did beseech.
'A pleasant walk, a pleasant talk,
　　Along the briny beach:
We cannot do with more than four,
　　To give a hand to each.'

The eldest Oyster looked at him,
　　But not a word he said:
The eldest Oyster winked his eye,
　　And shook his heavy head –
Meaning to say he did not choose
　　To leave the oyster-bed.

But four young Oysters hurried up,
　　All eager for the treat:
Their coats were brushed, their faces washed,
　　Their shoes were clean and neat –
And this was odd, because, you know,
　　They hadn't any feet.

Four other Oysters followed them,
　　And yet another four;
And thick and fast they came at last,
　　And more, and more, and more –
All hopping through the frothy waves,
　　And scrambling to the shore.

The Walrus and the Carpenter
    Walked on a mile or so,
And then they rested on a rock
    Conveniently low:
And all the little Oysters stood
    And waited in a row.

'The time has come,' the Walrus said,
    'To talk of many things:
Of shoes – and ships – and sealing-wax –
    Of cabbages – and kings –
And why the sea is boiling hot –
    And whether pigs have wings.'

'But wait a bit,' the Oysters cried,
    'Before we have our chat;
For some of us are out of breath,
    And all of us are fat!'
'No hurry!' cried the Carpenter.
    They thanked him much for that.

'A loaf of bread,' the Walrus said,
  'Is what we chiefly need:
Pepper and vinegar besides
  Are very good indeed –
Now, if you're ready, Oysters dear,
  We can begin to feed.'

'But not on us!' the Oysters cried,
  Turning a little blue.
'After such kindness that would be
  A dismal thing to do!'
'The night is fine,' the Walrus said.
  'Do you admire the view?

'It was so kind of you to come,
  And you are very nice!'
The Carpenter said nothing but
  'Cut us another slice.
I wish you were not quite so deaf –
  I've had to ask you twice!'

'It seems a shame,' the Walrus said,
  'To play them such a trick.
After we've brought them out so far,
  And made them trot so quick!'
The Carpenter said nothing but
  'The butter's spread too thick!'

'I weep for you,' the Walrus said:
  'I deeply sympathize.'
With sobs and tears he sorted out
  Those of the largest size,
Holding his pocket-handkerchief
  Before his streaming eyes.

'O Oysters,' said the Carpenter,
   'You've had a pleasant run!
Shall we be trotting home again?'
   But answer came there none —
And this was scarcely odd, because
   They'd eaten every one.

LEWIS CARROLL

Tom and His Pony, Jack

Tom had a little pony, Jack:
He vaulted lightly on its back
And galloped off for miles and miles,
A-leaping hedges, gates and stiles,
And shouting 'Yoicks!' and 'Tally-ho!'
And 'Heads I win!' and 'Tails below!'
And many another sporting phrase.
He rode like this for several days,
Until the pony, feeling tired,
Collapsed, looked heavenward and expired.
His father made a fearful row.
He said 'By Gum, you've done it now!
Here lies — a carcase on the ground —
No less than five and twenty pound!
Indeed the value of the beast
Would probably have much increased.
His teeth were false; and all were told
That he was only four years old.
Oh! Curse it all! I tell you plain
I'll never let you ride again.'

MORAL

His father died when he was twenty
And left three horses, which is plenty.

HILAIRE BELLOC

Jack and His Pony, Tom

Jack had a little pony — Tom;
He frequently would take it from
The stable where it used to stand
And give it sugar with his hand.
He also gave it oats and hay
And carrots twenty times a day
And grass in basketfuls, and greens
And Swedes and mangolds also beans
And patent foods from various sources
And bread (which isn't good for horses)
And chocolate and apple-rings
And lots and lots of other things
The most of which do not agree
With polo Ponies such as he.
And all in such a quantity
As ruined his digestion wholly
And turned him from a Ponopoly
— I mean a Polo Pony — into
A case that clearly must be seen to.
Because he swelled and swelled and swelled.
Which, when the kindly boy beheld,
He gave him medicine by the pail
And malted milk, and nutmeg ale,
And yet it only swelled the more
Until its stomach touched the floor,
And then it heaved and groaned as well
And staggered, till at last it fell

And found it could not rise again.
Jack wept and prayed — but all in vain.
The pony died, and as it died
Kicked him severely in the side.

MORAL

Kindness to animals should be
Attuned to their brutality.

HILAIRE BELLOC

The Song of Tyrannosaurus Rex

I'm a rock, I'm a mountain, I'm a hammer and a nail
I'm an army and a navy, I'm a force ten gale

I'm a trooper, I'm a tearaway, and time will never see
Another king, or anything, that fights like me

I'm a sinner, I'm a winner, I'm a one-man government
I'm the will of the people, I'm the force that's never spent

I'm a business and a factory, the work-force and the boss
I'm the brains and the belly and I never make a loss

I'm a monumental mason and the gravestones that I make
Are carved of flesh and bone from the carcases I take

I'm a god, I'm a ghost, I'm the creak on the stairs
I'm the grin that listens in when people say their prayers

I'm a crane, I'm a lorry, I'm a brand-new motorway
I set like concrete and I'm here to stay

O I'm big and I'm bad and I'm bold and I'm free
And the world will never see another villain like me

For I swagger and I swallow and the earth is my hotel
And I chew my meat in heaven and I lash my tail in hell!

WILLIAM SCAMMELL

Granny Boot

Granny in her bed one night
Heard a little squeak!
And then a little
Peck-peck-peck
Like something with a beak
Then something that went Binkle-Bonk
Ickle-tickle-toot
And all of it was coming
From inside Grandma's boot!
Then the boot began to *hop*
It went into the hall
And then from deep inside the boot
Came a Tarzan call
The sound of roaring lions
The screech of a cockatoo
Today that boot is in a cage
Locked in the London Zoo.

SPIKE MILLIGAN

Fishes' Nightsong

‿

‿   ‿

⏜   ⏜   ⏜

‿   ‿   ‿   ‿

⏜   ⏜   ⏜

‿   ‿   ‿   ‿

⏜   ⏜   ⏜

‿   ‿   ‿   ‿

⏜   ⏜   ⏜

‿   ‿   ‿   ‿

⏜   ⏜   ⏜

‿   ‿

‿

CHRISTIAN MORGENSTERN

IF YOU WAKE
AT MIDNIGHT

A Smuggler's Song

If you wake at midnight, and hear a horse's feet,
Don't go drawing back the blind, or looking in the street,
Them that asks no questions isn't told a lie,
Watch the wall, my darling, while the Gentlemen go by!
      Five and twenty ponies
      Trotting through the dark –
      Brandy for the Parson,
      'Baccy for the Clerk;
      Laces for a lady, letters for a spy,
And watch the wall, my darling, while the Gentlemen go by!

Running round the woodlump if you chance to find
Little barrels, roped and tarred, all full of brandy-wine,
Don't you shout to come and look, nor use 'em for your play.
Put the brushwood back again – and they'll be gone next day!

If you see the stable-door setting open wide;
If you see a tired horse lying down inside;
If your mother mends a coat cut about and tore;
If the lining's wet and warm – don't you ask no more!

If you meet King George's men, dressed in blue and red,
You be careful what you say, and mindful what is said.
If they call you 'pretty maid', and chuck you 'neath the chin,
Don't you tell where no-one is, nor yet where no-one's been!

Knocks and footsteps round the house — whistles after dark —
You've no call for running out till the house-dogs bark.
Trusty's here, and *Pincher*'s here, and see how dumb they lie —
They don't fret to follow when the Gentlemen go by!

If you do as you've been told, likely there's a chance
You'll be give a dainty doll, all the way from France,
With a cap of Valenciennes, and a velvet hood —
A present from the Gentlemen, along o' being good!
       Five and twenty ponies
       Trotting through the dark —
       Brandy for the Parson,
       'Baccy for the Clerk,
Them that asks no questions isn't told a lie —
Watch the wall, my darling, while the Gentlemen go by!

RUDYARD KIPLING

Flannan Isle

'Though three men dwell on Flannan Isle
To keep the lamp alight,
As we steered under the lee, we caught
No glimmer through the night.' —

A passing ship at dawn had brought
The news; and quickly we set sail,
To find out what strange thing might ail
The keepers of the deep-sea light.

The Winter day broke blue and bright,
With glancing sun and glancing spray,
While o'er the swell our boat made way,
As gallant as a gull in flight.

But as we neared the lonely Isle,
And looked up at the naked height,
And saw the lighthouse towering white,
With blinded lantern, that all night
Had never shot a spark
Of comfort through the dark,
So ghostly in the cold sunlight
It seemed, that we were struck the while
With wonder all too dread for words.

And as into the tiny creek
We stole beneath the hanging crag,
We saw three queer, black, ugly birds —
Too big, by far, in my belief,
For cormorant or shag —
Like seamen sitting bolt-upright
Upon a half-tide reef:
But, as we neared, they plunged from sight
Without a sound, or spurt of white.

And still too mazed to speak,
We landed; and made fast the boat;
And climbed the track in single file,
Each wishing he were safe afloat,
On any sea, however far,
So it be far from Flannan Isle:
And still we seemed to climb, and climb,
As though we'd lost all count of time,
And so must climb for evermore.
Yet, all too soon, we reached the door,
The black, sun-blistered lighthouse-door,
That gaped for us ajar.

As, on the threshold, for a spell,
We paused, we seemed to breathe the smell
Of limewash and of tar,
Familiar as our daily breath,
As though 'twere some strange scent of death:
And so, yet wondering, side by side,
We stood a moment, still tongue-tied:
And each with black foreboding eyed
The door, ere we should fling it wide,
To leave the sunlight for the gloom;

Till, plucking courage up, at last,
Hard on each other's heels we passed
Into the living-room.

Yet, as we crowded through the door,
We only saw a table, spread
For dinner, meat and cheese and bread;
But all untouched; and no-one there:
As though, when they sat down to eat,
Ere they could even taste,
Alarm had come; and they in haste
Had risen and left the bread and meat:
For at the table-head a chair
Lay tumbled on the floor.
We listened; but we only heard
The feeble cheeping of a bird
That starved upon its perch:
And, listening still, without a word,
We set about our hopeless search.

We hunted high, we hunted low;
And soon ransacked the empty house;
Then o'er the Island, to and fro,
We ranged, to listen and to look
In every cranny, cleft or nook
That might have hid a bird or mouse:
But, though we searched from shore to shore,
We found no sign in any place:
And soon again stood face to face
Before the gaping door:
And stole into the room once more
As frightened children steal.
Ay: though we hunted high and low,
And hunted everywhere,
Of the three men's fate we found no trace
Of any kind in any place:
But a door ajar, and an untouched meal,
And an overtoppled chair.

And as we listened in the gloom
Of that forsaken living-room —
A chill clutch on our breath —
We thought how ill-chance came to all
Who kept the Flannan Light:
And how the rock had been the death
Of many a likely lad:
How six had come to a sudden end,
And three had gone stark mad:
And one whom we'd all known as friend
Had leapt from the lantern one still night
And fallen dead by the lighthouse wall:
And long we thought
On the thing we sought,
And of what might yet befall.

Like curs a glance has brought to heel,
We listened, flinching there:
And looked, and looked, on the untouched meal,
And the overtoppled chair.

We seemed to stand for an endless while,
Though still no word was said,
Three men alive on Flannan Isle,
Who thought on three men dead.

WILFRID GIBSON

In the Stump of the Old Tree

In the stump of the old tree, where the heart has rotted out, / there is a hole the length of a man's arm, and a dank pool at the / bottom of it where the rain gathers, and the old leaves turn into / lacy skeletons. But do not put your hand down to see, because

in the stumps of old trees, where the hearts have rotted out, / there are holes the length of a man's arm, and dank pools at the / bottom where the rain gathers and old leaves turn to lace, and the / beak of a dead bird gapes like a trap. But do not put your / hand down to see, because

in the stumps of old trees with rotten hearts, where the rain / gathers and the laced leaves and the dead bird like a trap, there / are holes the length of a man's arm, and in every crevice of the / rotten wood grow weasels' eyes like molluscs, their lids open and shut with the tide. But do not put your hand down to see, because

in the stumps of old trees where the rain gathers and the / trapped leaves and the beak, and the laced weasel's eyes, there are / holes the length of a man's arm, and at the bottom a sodden bible / written in the language of rooks. But do not put your hand down / to see, because

in the stumps of old trees where the hearts have rotted out there are holes the length of a man's arm where the weasels are / trapped and the letters of the rook language are laced on the / sodden leaves, and at the bottom there is a man's arm. But do / not put your hand down to see, because

in the stumps of old trees where the hearts have rotted out / there are deep holes and dank pools where the rain gathers, and / if you ever put your hand down to see, you can wipe it in the / sharp grass till it bleeds, but you'll never want to eat with / it again.

HUGH SYKES-DAVIES

A Case of Murder

They should not have left him there alone,
Alone that is except for the cat.
He was only nine, not old enough
To be left alone in a basement flat,
Alone, that is, except for the cat.
A dog would have been a different thing,
A big gruff dog with slashing jaws,
But a cat with round eyes mad as gold,
Plump as a cushion with tucked-in paws —
Better have left him with a fair-sized rat!
But what they did was leave him with a cat.
He hated that cat; he watched it sit,
A buzzing machine of soft black stuff,
He sat and watched and he hated it,
Snug in its fur, hot blood in a muff,
And its mad gold stare and the way it sat
Crooning dark warmth: he loathed all that.
So he took Daddy's stick and he hit the cat.
Then quick as a sudden crack in glass
It hissed, black flash, to a hiding place
In the dust and dark beneath the couch,
And he followed the grin on his new-made face,
A wide-eyed, frightened snarl of a grin,
And he took the stick and he thrust it in,
Hard and quick in the furry dark,
The black fur squealed and he felt his skin
Prickle with sparks of dry delight.
Then the cat again came into sight,

Shot for the door that wasn't quite shut,
But the boy, quick too, slammed fast the door:
The cat, half-through, was cracked like a nut
And the soft black thud was dumped on the floor.
Then the boy was suddenly terrified
And he bit his knuckles and cried and cried;
But he had to do something with the dead thing there.
His eyes squeezed beads of salty prayer
But the wound of fear gaped wide and raw;
He dared not touch the thing with his hands
So he fetched a spade and shovelled it
And dumped the load of heavy fur
In the spidery cupboard under the stair
Where it's been for years, and though it died
It's grown in that cupboard and its hot low purr
Grows slowly louder year by year:
There'll not be a corner for the boy to hide
When the cupboard swells and all sides split
And the huge black cat pads out of it.

VERNON SCANNELL

A Book of Ghosts

An author wrote a book on ghosts,
A ghost a page, a shiver a line,
His spooks were terribly gaunt and grim,
A ghost a page, a shiver a line,
The ghosts were grim but the sales were fine.

The author sat alone one night,
A ghost a page, a shiver a line,
He dined alone in his cold damp room,
A ghost a page, a shiver a line,
The hands said eight but the clock struck nine.

He calmly invented another grim ghoul,
A ghost a page, a shiver a line,
Nor knew that a ghost stood hard by his arm,
A ghost a page, a shiver a line,
But ate, and drank of the fruit of the vine.

The ghost breathed deeply into his ear,
A ghost a page, a shiver a line,
And pulled his hair and flicked his nose,
A ghost a page, a shiver a line,
His dinner-plate rose as it sat down to dine.

The author's eyes popped out of his head,
A ghost a page, a shiver a line,
His wine-glass flew towards the door,
A ghost a page, a shiver a line,
A ghostly shiver ran down his spine.

Ten ice-cold fingers clutched his throat,
A ghost a page, a shiver a line,
Ten lightning flashes burned his brain,
A ghost a page, a shiver a line,
He writes no more, and drinks no wine.

PHILIP ENNIS

The Old Wife and the Ghost

There was an old wife and she lived all alone
   In a cottage not far from Hitchin:
And one bright night, by the full moon light,
   Comes a ghost right into her kitchen.

About that kitchen neat and clean
   The ghost goes pottering round.
But the poor old wife is deaf as a boot
   And so hears never a sound.

The ghost blows up the kitchen fire,
   As bold as bold can be;
He helps himself from the larder shelf,
   But never a sound hears she.

He blows on his hands to make them warm,
   And whistles aloud 'Whee-hee!'
But still as a sack the old soul lies
   And never a sound hears she.

From corner to corner he runs about,
   And into the cupboard he peeps;
He rattles the door and bumps on the floor,
   But still the old wife sleeps.

Jangle and bang go the pots and pans,
   As he throws them all around;
And the plates and mugs and dishes and jugs,
   He flings them all to the ground.

Madly the ghost tears up and down
  And screams like a storm at sea;
And at last the old wife stirs in her bed –
  And it's 'Drat those mice,' says she.

Then the first cock crows and morning shows
  And the troublesome ghost's away.
But oh! what a pickle the poor wife sees
  When she gets up next day.

'Them's tidy big mice,' the old wife thinks,
  And off she goes to Hitchin,
And a tidy big cat she fetches back
  To keep the mice from her kitchen.

                              JAMES REEVES

Colonel Fazackerley

Colonel Fazackerley Butterworth-Toast
Bought an old castle complete with a ghost,
But someone or other forgot to declare
To Colonel Fazack that the spectre was there.

On the very first evening, while waiting to dine,
The Colonel was taking a fine sherry wine,
When the ghost, with a furious flash and a flare,
Shot out of the chimney and shivered 'Beware!'

Colonel Fazackerley put down his glass
And said, 'My dear fellow, that's really first class!
I just can't conceive how you do it at all.
I imagine you're going to a Fancy Dress Ball?'

At this, the dread ghost gave a withering cry.
Said the Colonel (his monocle firm in his eye),
'Now just how you do it I wish I could think.
Do sit down and tell me, and please have a drink.'

The ghost in his phosphorous cloak gave a roar
And floated about between ceiling and floor.
He walked through a wall and returned through a pane
And backed up the chimney and came down again.

Said the Colonel, 'With laughter I'm feeling quite weak!'
(As trickles of merriment ran down his cheek).
'My house-warming party I hope you won't spurn.
You *must* say you'll come and you'll give us a turn!'

At this, the poor spectre – quite out of his wits –
Proceeded to shake himself almost to bits.
He rattled his chains and he clattered his bones
And he filled the whole castle with mumbles and groans.

But Colonel Fazackerley, just as before,
Was simply delighted and called out, 'Encore!'
At which the ghost vanished, his efforts in vain,
And never was seen at the castle again.

'Oh dear, what a pity!' said Colonel Fazack.
'I don't know his name, so I won't call him back.'
And then with a smile that was hard to define,
Colonel Fazackerley went in to dine.

CHARLES CAUSLEY

Jabberwocky

(from *Through the Looking-Glass*)

'Twas brillig, and the slithy toves
   Did gyre and gimble in the wabe;
All mimsy were the borogoves,
   And the mome raths outgrabe.

'Beware the Jabberwock, my son!
   The jaws that bite, the claws that catch!
Beware the Jubjub bird, and shun
   The frumious Bandersnatch!'

He took his vorpal sword in hand:
   Long time the manxome foe he sought –
So rested he by the Tumtum tree,
   And stood awhile in thought.

And as in uffish thought he stood,
   The Jabberwock, with eyes of flame,
Came whiffling through the tulgey wood,
   And burbled as it came!

One, two! One, two! And through and through
    The vorpal blade went snicker-snack!
He left it dead, and with its head
    He went galumphing back.

'And hast thou slain the Jabberwock?
    Come to my arms, my beamish boy!
O frabjous day! Callooh! Callay!'
    He chortled in his joy.

'Twas brillig, and the slithy toves
    Did gyre and gimble in the wabe;
All mimsy were the borogoves,
    And the mome raths outgrabe.

LEWIS CARROLL

The Ghoul

The gruesome ghoul, the grisly ghoul,
without the slightest noise
waits patiently beside the school
to feast on girls and boys.

He lunges fiercely through the air
as they come out to play,
then grabs a couple by the hair
and drags them far away.

He cracks their bones and snaps their backs
and squeezes out their lungs,
he chews their thumbs like candy snacks
and pulls apart their tongues.

He slices their stomachs and bites their hearts
and tears their flesh to shreds,
he swallows their toes like toasted tarts
and gobbles down their heads.

Fingers, elbows, hands and knees
and arms and legs and feet –
he eats them with delight and ease,
for every part's a treat.

And when the gruesome, grisly ghoul
has nothing left to chew,
he hurries to another school
and waits ... perhaps for you.

JACK PRELUTSKY

Alternative Endings
to an Unwritten Ballad

I stole through the dungeons, while everyone slept,
Till I came to the cage where the Monster was kept.
There, locked in the arms of a Giant Baboon,
Rigid and smiling, lay ... MRS RAVOON!

I climbed the clock tower in the first morning sun
And 'twas midday at least 'ere my journey was done;
But the clock never sounded the last stroke of noon,
For there, from the clapper, swung MRS RAVOON!

I hauled in the line, and I took my first look
At the half-eaten horror that hung from the hook.
I had dragged from the depths of the limpid lagoon
The luminous body of MRS RAVOON.

I fled in the storm, the lightning and thunder,
And there, as a flash split the darkness asunder,
Chewing a rat's-tail and mumbling a rune,
Mad in the moat squatted MRS RAVOON!

I stood by the waters so green and so thick,
And I stirred at the scum with my old, withered stick;
When there rose through the ooze, like a monstrous balloon,
The bloated cadaver of MRS RAVOON.

Facing the fens, I looked back from the shore
Where all had been empty a moment before;
And there by the light of the Lincolnshire moon,
Immense on the marshes, stood ... MRS RAVOON!

PAUL DEHN

The Dong with a Luminous Nose

When awful darkness and silence reign
Over the great Gromboolian plain,
   Through the long, long wintry nights –
When the angry breakers roar
As they beat on the rocky shore –
   When Storm-clouds brood on the towering heights
Of the Hills of the Chankly Bore –

Then, through the vast and gloomy dark,
There moves what seems a fiery spark,
   A lonely spark with silvery rays
   Piercing the coal-black night –
   A Meteor strange and bright –
Hither and thither the vision strays,
   A single lurid light.

Slowly it wanders – pauses – creeps –
Anon it sparkles – flashes and leaps;
And ever as onward it gleaming goes
A light on the Bong-tree stems it throws.
And those who watch at that midnight hour
From Hall or Terrace, or lofty Tower,
Cry, as the wild light passes along –
     'The Dong! – the Dong!
  'The wandering Dong through the forest goes!
    'The Dong! the Dong!
  'The Dong with a luminous Nose!'

Long years ago
The Dong was happy and gay,
Till he fell in love with a Jumbly Girl
Who came to those shores one day,
For the Jumblies came in a sieve, they did –
Landing at eve near the Zemmery Fidd
Where the Oblong Oysters grow,
And the rocks are smooth and gray.
And all the woods and the valleys rang
With the Chorus they daily and nightly sang –
'Far and few, far and few,
Are the lands where the Jumblies live;
Their heads are green, and their hands are blue
And they went to sea in a sieve.'

Happily, happily passed those days!
While the cheerful Jumblies staid;
They danced in circlets all night long,
To the plaintive pipe of the lively Dong,
In moonlight, shine, or shade.
For day and night he was always there
By the side of the Jumbly Girl so fair,
With her sky-blue hands, and her sea-green hair.
Till the morning came of that hateful day
When the Jumblies sailed in their sieve away,
And the Dong was left on the cruel shore
Gazing – gazing for evermore –
Ever keeping his weary eyes on
That pea-green sail on the far horizon –
Singing the Jumbly Chorus still
As he sate all day on the grassy hill –

'Far and few, far and few,
Are the lands where the Jumblies live;
Their heads are green, and their hands are blue,
And they went to sea in a sieve.'

But when the sun was low in the West,
   The Dong arose and said –
   'What little sense I once possessed
   Has quite gone out of my head!' –
And since that day he wanders still
By lake and forest, marsh and hill,
Singing – 'O somewhere, in valley or plain
'Might I find my Jumbly Girl again!
'For ever I'll seek by lake and shore
'Till I find my Jumbly Girl once more!'

     Playing a pipe with silvery squeaks,
     Since then his Jumbly Girl he seeks,
     And because by night he could not see,
     He gathered the bark of the Twangum Tree
       On the flowery plain that grows.
       And he wove him a wondrous Nose –
     A Nose as strange as a Nose could be!
Of vast proportions and painted red,
And tied with cords to the back of his head.
     – In a hollow rounded space it ended
     With a luminous Lamp within suspended,
       All fenced about
       With a bandage stout
       To prevent the wind from blowing it out –
     And with holes all round to send the light,
     In gleaming rays on the dismal night.

And now each night, and all night long,
Over those plains still roams the Dong;
And above the wail of the Chimp and Snipe
You may hear the squeak of his plaintive pipe
While ever he seeks, but seeks in vain
To meet with his Jumbly Girl again;
Lonely and wild – all night he goes –
The Dong with a luminous Nose!
And all who watch at the midnight hour,
From Hall or Terrace, or lofty Tower,
Cry, as they trace the Meteor bright,
Moving along through the dreary night –
　　　　'This is the hour when forth he goes,
　　　　'The Dong with a luminous Nose!
　　　　'Yonder – over the plain he goes;
　　　　　'He goes!
　　　　　'He goes;
　　　'The Dong with a luminous Nose!'

EDWARD LEAR

A BUNCH
OF THE BOYS

The Highwayman

PART ONE

The wind was a torrent of darkness among the gusty trees,
The moon was a ghostly galleon tossed upon cloudy seas,
The road was a ribbon of moonlight over the purple moor,
And the highwayman came riding –
    Riding – riding –
The highwayman came riding, up to the old inn-door.
He'd a French cocked-hat on his forehead, a bunch of lace at his chin,
A coat of the claret velvet, and breeches of brown doeskin:
They fitted with never a wrinkle; his boots were up to the thigh!
And he rode with a jewelled twinkle,
    His pistol butts a-twinkle,
His rapier hilt a-twinkle, under the jewelled sky.

Over the cobbles he clattered and clashed in the dark inn-yard,
And he tapped with his whip on the shutters, but all was locked and
      barred:
He whistled a tune to the window; and who should be waiting there
But the landlord's black-eyed daughter,
    Bess, the landlord's daughter,
Plaiting a dark red love-knot into her long black hair.

And dark in the dark old inn-yard a stable-wicket creaked
Where Tim, the ostler, listened; his face was white and peaked,
His eyes were hollows of madness, his hair like mouldy hay;
But he loved the landlord's daughter,
    The landlord's red-lipped daughter:
Dumb as a dog he listened, and he heard the robber say —

'One kiss, my bonny sweetheart, I'm after a prize tonight,
But I shall be back with the yellow gold before the morning light.
Yet if they press me sharply, and harry me through the day,
Then look for me by moonlight,
    Watch for me by moonlight:
I'll come to thee by moonlight, though Hell should bar the way.'

He rose upright in the stirrups, he scarce could reach her hand;
But she loosened her hair i'the casement! His face burnt like a brand
As the black cascade of perfume came tumbling over his breast;
And he kissed its waves in the moonlight,
    (Oh, sweet black waves in the moonlight)
Then he tugged at his reins in the moonlight, and galloped away to
        the West.

PART TWO

He did not come in the dawning, he did not come at noon;
And out of the tawny sunset, before the rise o' the moon,
When the road was a gypsy's ribbon, looping the purple moor,
A red-coat troop came marching –
    Marching – marching –
King George's men came marching, up to the old inn-door.

They said no word to the landlord, they drank his ale instead;
But they gagged his daughter and bound her to the foot of her narrow
        bed.
Two of them knelt at her casement, with muskets at the side!
There was death at every window;
    And Hell at one dark window;
For Bess could see, through her casement, the road that *he* would ride.

They had tied her up to attention, with many a sniggering jest:
They had bound a musket beside her, with the barrel beneath her breast!
'Now keep good watch!' and they kissed her.
    She heard the dead man say –
Look for me by moonlight;
    Watch for me by moonlight;
I'll come to thee by moonlight, though Hell should bar the way!

She twisted her hands behind her; but all the knots held good!
She writhed her hands till her fingers were wet with sweat or blood!
They stretched and strained in the darkness, and the hours crawled by
      like years;
Till, now, on the stroke of midnight,
    Cold, on the stroke of midnight,
The tip of one finger touched it! The trigger at least was hers!

103

The tip of one finger touched it; she strove no more for the rest!
Up, she stood up to attention, with the barrel beneath her breast,
She would not risk their hearing: she would not strive again;
For the road lay bare in the moonlight,
     Blank and bare in the moonlight;
And the blood of her veins in the moonlight throbbed to her Love's
          refrain.

Tlot-tlot, tlot-tlot! Had they heard it? The horse-hoofs ringing clear –
Tlot-tlot, tlot-tlot, in the distance? Were they deaf that they did not
          hear?
Down the ribbon of moonlight, over the brow of the hill,
The highwayman came riding,
     Riding, riding!
The red-coats looked to their priming! She stood up straight and still!

Tlot-tlot, in the frosty silence! *Tlot-tlot* in the echoing night!
Nearer he came and nearer! Her face was like a light!
Her eyes grew wide for a moment; she drew one last deep breath,
Then her finger moved in the moonlight,
     Her musket shattered the moonlight,
Shattered her breast in the moonlight and warned him – with her
          death.

He turned; he spurred him westward; he did not know who stood
Bowed with her head o'er the musket, drenched with her own red
          blood!
Not till the dawn he heard it, and slowly blanched to hear
How Bess, the landlord's daughter,
     The landlord's black-eyed daughter,
Had watched for her Love in the moonlight; and died in the darkness
          there.

Back, he spurred like a madman, shrieking a curse to the sky,
With the white road smoking behind him, and his rapier brandished
   high!
Blood-red were his spurs i'the golden noon; wine-red was his velvet
   coat;
When they shot him down on the highway,
   Down like a dog on the highway,
And he lay in his blood on the highway, with the bunch of lace at his
   throat.

*

And still of a winter's night, they say, when the wind is in the trees,
When the moon is a ghostly galleon tossed upon cloudy seas,
When the road is a ribbon of moonlight over the purple moor,
A highwayman comes riding —
   Riding — riding —
A highwayman comes riding, up to the old inn-door.

Over the cobbles he clatters and clangs in the dark inn-yard;
And he taps with his whip on the shutters, but all is locked and barred:
He whistles a tune to the window, and who should be waiting there
But the landlord's black-eyed daughter,
   Bess, the landlord's daughter,
Plaiting a dark red love-knot into her long black hair.

ALFRED NOYES

The Shooting of Dan McGrew

A bunch of the boys were whooping it up in the Malamute saloon;
The kid that handles the music-box was hitting a rag-time tune;
Back of the bar, in a solo game, sat Dangerous Dan McGrew,
And watching his luck was his light o' love, the lady that's known
as Lou.

When out of the night, which was fifty below, and into the din and
the glare,
There stumbled a miner fresh from the creeks, dog-dirty and loaded
for bear.
He looked like a man with a foot in the grave, and scarcely the strength
of a louse,
Yet he tilted a poke of dust on the bar, and he called for drinks on
the house.
There was none could place the stranger's face, though we searched
ourselves for a clue;
But we drank his health, and the last to drink was Dangerous Dan
McGrew.

There's men that somehow just grip your eyes, and hold them hard
like a spell;
And such was he, and he looked at me like a man who had lived in
hell;
With a face most hair, and the dreary stare of a dog whose day is done,
As he watered the green stuff in his glass, and the drops fell one by one.
Then I got to figgering who he was, and wondering what he'd do,
And I turned my head – and there watching him was the lady that's
known as Lou.

His eyes went rubbering round the room, and he seemed in a kind of
daze,
Till at last that old piano fell in the way of his wandering gaze.
The rag-time kid was having a drink; there was no-one else on the
stool,
So the stranger stumbles across the room, and flops down there like
a fool.
In a buckskin shirt that was glazed with dirt he sat, and I saw him sway;
Then he clutched the keys with his talon hands – my God! but that
man could play!

Were you ever out in the Great Alone, when the moon was awful clear,
And the icy mountains hemmed you in with a silence you most could
hear;
With only the howl of a timber wolf, and you camped there in the cold,
A half-dead thing in a stark, dead world, clean mad for the muck called
gold;
While high overhead, green, yellow, and red, the North Lights swept
in bars –
Then you've a hunch what the music meant ... hunger and night and
the stars.

And hunger not of the belly kind, that's banished with bacon and
beans;
But the gnawing hunger of lonely men for a home and all that it means;
For a fireside far from the cares that are, four walls and a roof above;
But oh! so cramful of cosy joy, and crowned with a woman's love;
A woman dearer than all the world, and true as Heaven is true –
(God! how ghastly she looks through her rouge – the lady that's
known as Lou.)

Then on a sudden the music changed, so soft that you scarce could
    hear;
But you felt that your life had been looted clean of all that it once
    held dear;
That someone had stolen the woman you loved; that her love was a
    devil's lie;
That your guts were gone, and the best for you was to crawl away
    and die.
'Twas the crowning cry of a heart's despair, and it thrilled you through
    and through –
'I guess I'll make it a spread misere,' said Dangerous Dan McGrew.

The music almost died away ... then it burst like a pent-up flood;
And it seemed to say, 'Repay, repay,' and my eyes were blind with
    blood.
The thought came back of an ancient wrong, and it stung like a
    frozen lash,
And the lust awoke to kill, to kill ... then the music stopped with
    a crash,
And the stranger turned, and his eyes they burned in a most peculiar
    way;
In a buckskin shirt that was glazed with dirt he sat, and I saw him sway;
Then his lips went in in a kind of grin, and he spoke, and his voice
    was calm;
And, 'Boys,' says he, 'you don't know me, and none of you care a
    damn;
But I want to state, and my words are straight, and I'll bet my poke
    they're true,
That one of you is a hound of hell ... and that one is Dan McGrew.'

Then I ducked my head, and the lights went out, and two guns blazed
    in the dark;

And a woman screamed, and the lights went up, and two men lay stiff
    and stark;

Pitched on his head, and pumped full of lead, was Dangerous Dan
    McGrew,

While the man from the creeks lay clutched to the breast of the lady
    that's known as Lou.

These are the simple facts of the case, and I guess I ought to know;

They say that the stranger was crazed with 'hooch', and I'm not
    denying it's so.

I'm not so wise as the lawyer guys, but strictly between us two –

The woman that kissed him – and pinched his poke – was the lady
    that's known as Lou.

ROBERT W. SERVICE

The Last Song of Billy the Kid

I'll tell you the story of Billy the Kid.
I'll tell of the things that this young outlaw did
Way out in the West when the country was young,
When the gun was the law and the law was a gun.

Now the Mexican maidens play gúitars and sing
Songs about Billy, the boy bandit-king
But with drinkin' and gamblin' he come to his end,
Shot down by Pat Garrett who once was his friend.

Pat Garrett rode up to the window that night,
The desert was still and the moonlight was bright,
Pat listened outside while the Kid told his tale
Of shooting the guard in the Las Cruces jail.

'I rode down the border and robbed in Juaréz,
I drank to the ladies the happiest of days,
My picture is posted from Texas to Maine
And women and ridin' and robbin's my game.'

All the while Billy bragged Pat waited outside.
Bill said to his friends, 'I ain't satisfied.
Twenty-one men I have put bullets through,
The sheriff, Pat Garrett, must make twenty-two.'

Then Pat Garrett fired and his thumb-buster cracked.
Billy fell dead, he was blowed through the back.
Pat rode away, left the Kid lying dead,
And this is the last song of Billy the Kid.

ANON.

The White Knight's Song

(from *Through the Looking-Glass*)

I'll tell thee everything I can;
    There's little to relate.
I saw an aged aged man,
    A-sitting on a gate.
'Who are you, aged man?' I said,
    'And how is it you live?'
And his answer trickled through my head
    Like water through a sieve.

He said 'I look for butterflies
    That sleep among the wheat:
I make them into mutton-pies,
    And sell them in the street.
I sell them unto men,' he said,
    'Who sail on stormy seas;
And that's the way I get my bread –
    A trifle, if you please.'

But I was thinking of a plan
    To dye one's whiskers green,
And always use so large a fan
    That they could not be seen.
So, having no reply to give
    To what the old man said,
I cried 'Come, tell me how you live!'
    And thumped him on the head.

His accents mild took up the tale:
   He said 'I go my ways,
And when I find a mountain-rill,
   I set it in a blaze;
And thence they make a stuff they call
   Rowland's Macassar-Oil —
Yet twopence-halfpenny is all
   They give me for my toil.'

But I was thinking of a way
   To feed oneself on batter,
And so go on from day to day
   Getting a little fatter.
I shook him well from side to side,
   Until his face was blue:
'Come, tell me how you live,' I cried,
   'And what it is you do!'

He said 'I hunt for haddocks' eyes
   Among the heather bright,
And work them into waistcoat-buttons
   In the silent night.
And these I do not sell for gold
   Or coin of silvery shine,
But for a copper halfpenny,
   And that will purchase nine.

'I sometimes dig for buttered rolls,
   Or set limed twigs for crabs;
I sometimes search the grassy knolls
   For wheels of Hansom-cabs.
And that's the way' (he gave a wink)
   'By which I get my wealth —
And very gladly will I drink
   Your Honour's noble health.'

I heard him then, for I had just
   Completed my design
To keep the Menai bridge from rust
   By boiling it in wine.
I thanked him much for telling me
   The way he got his wealth,
But chiefly for his wish that he
   Might drink my noble health.

And now, if e'er by chance I put
   My fingers into glue,
Or madly squeeze a right-hand foot
   Into a left-hand shoe,
Or if I drop upon my toe
   A very heavy weight,
I weep, for it reminds me so
Of that old man I used to know –
Whose look was mild, whose speech was slow,
Whose hair was whiter than the snow,
Whose face was very like a crow,
With eyes, like cinders, all aglow,
Who seemed distracted with his woe,
Who rocked his body to and fro,
And muttered mumblingly and low,
As if his mouth were full of dough,
Who snorted like a buffalo –
That summer evening long ago,
   A-sitting on a gate.

LEWIS CARROLL

My Father

Some fathers work at the office, others work at the store,
Some operate great cranes and build up skyscrapers galore,
Some work in canning factories counting green peas into cans,
Some drive all night in huge and thundering removal vans.

    But mine has the strangest job of the lot.
    My Father's the Chief Inspector of – What?
    O don't tell the mice, don't tell the moles,
    My Father's the Chief Inspector of HOLES.

It's a work of the highest importance because you never know
What's in a hole, what fearful thing is creeping from below.
Perhaps it's a hole to the ocean and will soon gush water in tons,
Or maybe it leads to a vast cave full of gold and skeletons.

    Though a hole might seem to have nothing but dirt in,
    Somebody's simply got to make certain.
    Caves in the mountain, clefts in the wall,
    My Father has to inspect them all.

That crack in the road looks harmless. My Father knows it's not.
The world may be breaking into two and starting at that spot.
Or maybe the world is a great egg, and we live on the shell,
And it's just beginning to split and hatch: you simply cannot tell.

    If you see a crack, run to the phone, run!
    My Father will know just what's to be done.
    A rumbling hole, a silent hole,
    My Father will soon have it under control.

Keeping a check on all these holes he hurries from morning to night.
There might be sounds of marching in one, or an eye shining bright.
A tentacle came groping from a hole that belonged to a mouse,
A floor collapsed and Chinamen swarmed up into the house.

A Hole's an unpredictable thing –
Nobody knows what a Hole might bring.
Caves in the mountain, clefts in the wall,
My Father has to inspect them all!

TED HUGHES

Lord Hippo

Lord Hippo suffered fearful loss
By putting money on a horse
Which he believed, if it were pressed,
Would run far faster than the rest:
For someone who was in the know
Had confidently told him so.
But on the morning of the race
It only took the *seventh* place!
Picture the Viscount's great surprise!
He scarcely could believe his eyes!
He sought the Individual who
Had laid him odds at 9 to 2,
Suggesting as a useful tip
That they should enter Partnership
And put to joint account the debt
Arising from this foolish bet.
But when the Bookie – oh! my word,
I only wish you could have heard

The way he roared he did not think,
And hoped that they might strike him pink!
Lord Hippo simply turned and ran
From this infuriated man.
Despairing, maddened and distraught,
He utterly collapsed and sought
His sire, the Earl of Potamus,
And brokenly addressed him thus:
'Dread Sire – today – at Ascot – I ...'
His genial parent made reply:
'Come! Come! Come! Come! Don't look so glum!
Trust your Papa and name the sum ...
WHAT? *Fifteen hundred thousand?* ... Hum!
However ... stiffen up, you wreck;
Boys will be boys – so here's the cheque!'
Lord Hippo, feeling deeply – well,
More grateful than he cared to tell –
Punted the lot on Little Nell:
And got a telegram at dinner
To say that he had backed the Winner!

HILAIRE BELLOC

La Belle Dame sans Merci

'O what can ail thee, knight-at-arms,
  Alone and palely loitering?
The sedge has withered from the lake
  And no birds sing.

'O what can ail thee, knight-at-arms,
  So haggard and so woe-begone?
The squirrel's granary is full,
  And the harvest's done.

'I see a lily on thy brow
  With anguish moist and fever-dew,
And on thy cheeks a fading rose
  Fast withereth too.'

'I met a lady in the meads
  Full beautiful — a faery's child,
Her hair was long, her foot was light,
  And her eyes were wild.

'I made a garland for her head,
   And bracelets too, and fragrant zone;
She looked at me as she did love
   And made sweet moan.

'I set her on my pacing steed
   And nothing else saw all day long;
For sidelong would she bend, and sing
   A faery's song.

'She found me roots of relish sweet
   And honey wild and manna-dew;
And sure in language strange she said –
   "I love thee true."

'She took me to her elfin grot,
   And there she wept and sigh'd full sore,
And there I shut her wild wild eyes
   With kisses four.

'And there she lulled me asleep,
   And there I dreamed – Ah! woe betide! –
The latest dream I ever dream'd
   On the cold hill side.

'I saw pale kings, and princes too,
   Pale warriors, death-pale were they all;
They cried, "La Belle Dame sans Merci
   Thee hath in thrall!"

'I saw their starved lips in the gloam
　　With horrid warning gaped wide,
And I awoke and found me here
　　On the cold hill's side.

'And this is why I sojourn here
　　Alone and palely loitering,
Though the sedge is wither'd from the lake,
　　And no birds sing.'

JOHN KEATS

The Cruel Mother

She sat down below a thorn,
  Fine flowers in the valley,
And there she has her sweet babe born,
  And the green leaves they grow rarely.

'Smile na sae sweet, my bonnie babe,
An ye smile sae sweet, ye'll smile me dead.'

She's taen out her little pen-knife,
And twinn'd the sweet babe o' its life.

She's howket a grave by the light o' the moon,
And there she's buried her sweet babe in.

As she was going to the church,
She saw a sweet babe in the porch.

'O sweet babe, an thou were mine,
I wad cleed thee in the silk so fine.'

'O mother dear, when I was thine,'
  Fine flowers in the valley,
'You didna prove to me sae kind.'
  And the green leaves they grow rarely.

ANON.

Lord Ullin's Daughter

A chieftain, to the Highlands bound,
    Cries, 'Boatman, do not tarry!
And I'll give thee a silver pound
    To row us o'er the ferry.'

'Now who be ye, would cross Lochgyle,
    This dark and stormy water?'
'Oh, I'm the chief of Ulva's isle,
    And this Lord Ullin's daughter.

'And fast before her father's men
    Three days we've fled together;
For should he find us in the glen,
    My blood would stain the heather.

'His horsemen hard behind us ride;
    Should they our steps discover,
Then who will cheer my bonny bride
    When they have slain her lover?'

Out spoke the hardy Highland wight,
    'I'll go, my chief – I'm ready.
It is not for your silver bright,
    But for your winsome lady.

'And by my word! the bonny bird
    In danger shall not tarry;
So though the waves are raging white,
    I'll row you o'er the ferry.'

By this the storm grew loud apace;
    The water-wraith was shrieking;
And in the scowl of heaven each face
    Grew dark as they were speaking.

But still as wilder blew the wind,
    And as the night grew drearer,
Adown the glen rode armed men –
    Their trampling sounded nearer.

'O haste thee, haste!' the lady cries,
    'Though tempests round us gather;
I'll meet the raging of the skies,
    But not an angry father.'

The boat has left a stormy land,
    A stormy sea before her –
When, O! too strong for human hand,
    The tempest gathered o'er her.

And still they rowed amidst the roar
    Of waters fast prevailing –
Lord Ullin reached that fatal shore;
    His wrath was changed to wailing.

For sore dismayed through storm and shade
    His child he did discover;
One lovely hand she stretched for aid,
    And one was round her lover.

'Come back! come back!' he cried in grief,
   'Across this stormy water;
And I'll forgive your Highland chief,
   My daughter! – O my daughter!'

'Twas vain – the loud waves lashed the shore,
   Return or aid preventing.
The waters wild went o'er his child,
   And he was left lamenting.

THOMAS CAMPBELL

Three Fishers Went Sailing

Three fishers went sailing out into the West,
    Away to the West as the sun went down;
Each thought on the woman that loved him the best,
    And the children stood watching them out of the town:
For men must work, and women must weep,
And there's little to earn, and many to keep,
    Though the harbour-bar be moaning.

Three wives sat up in the lighthouse tower,
    And they trimmed their lamps as the sun went down;
And they looked at the squall and they looked at the shower,
    And the night-rack came rolling up ragged and brown;
But men must work, and women must weep,
Though storms be sudden, and waters deep,
    And the harbour-bar be moaning.

Three corpses lay out on the shining sands,
    In the morning gleam as the sun went down,
And the women are weeping and wringing their hands,
    For those who will never come back to the town.
For men must work, and women must weep,
And the sooner it's over, the sooner to sleep,
    And goodbye to the bar and its moaning.

CHARLES KINGSLEY

The Lady and the Gypsy

I handed her my silver
And gullibility,
And tremulously asked her
Who would marry me,
For I was getting older,
Approaching twenty-three –
At least that's what I told her:
All girls, I'm sure, agree
It's sometimes right to suffer
Lapse of memory.

She told me to be patient,
But not for very long,
For down the summer pavement
As lilting as a song
Mr Right would wander,
Eager, gallant, strong;
And sure enough last summer
My man did come along:
If he is Mr Right, then
Give me Mr Wrong.

VERNON SCANNELL

BATTLE ORDER

The Revenge. A Ballad of the Fleet

At Flores in the Azores Sir Richard Grenville lay,
And a pinnace, like a fluttered bird, came flying from far away;
'Spanish ships of war at sea! We have counted fifty-three!'
Then sware Lord Thomas Howard: ''Fore God I am no coward;
But I cannot meet them here, for my ships are out of gear,
And the half my men are sick. I must fly, but follow quick.
We are six ships of the line; can we fight with fifty-three?'

Then spake Sir Richard Grenville: 'I know you are no coward;
You fly them for a moment to fight with them again.
But I've ninety men and more that are lying sick ashore.
I should count myself the coward if I left them, my Lord Howard,
To these Inquisition dogs and the devildoms of Spain.'

So Lord Howard passed away with five ships of war that day,
Till he melted like a cloud in the silent summer heaven;
But Sir Richard bore in hand all his sick men from the land
Very carefully and slow,
Men of Bideford in Devon,
And we laid them on the ballast down below;
For we brought them all aboard,
And they blessed him in their pain, that they were not left to Spain,
To the thumbscrew and the stake, for the glory of the Lord.

He had only a hundred seamen to work the ship and to fight,
And he sailed away from Flores till the Spaniard came in sight,
With his huge sea-castles heaving upon the weather bow.
'Shall we fight or shall we fly?
Good Sir Richard, tell us now,
For to fight is but to die!
There'll be little of us left by the time this sun be set.'
And Sir Richard said again: 'We be all good English men.
Let us bang these dogs of Seville, the children of the devil,
For I never turned my back upon Don or devil yet.'

Sir Richard spoke and he laughed, and we roared a hurrah, and so
The little Revenge ran on sheer into the heart of the foe,
With her hundred fighters on deck, and her ninety sick below;
For half of their fleet to the right and half to the left were seen,
And the little Revenge ran on through the long sea-lane between.

Thousands of their soldiers looked down from their decks and laughed,
Thousands of their seamen made mock of the mad little craft
Running on and on, till delayed
By their mountain-like San Philip that, of fifteen hundred tons,
And up-shadowing high above us with her yawning tiers of guns,
Took the breath from our sails, and we stayed.

And while now the great San Philip hung above us like a cloud
Whence the thunderbolt will fall
Long and loud,
Four galleons drew away
From the Spanish fleet that day,
And two upon the larboard and two upon the starboard lay,
And the battle-thunder broke from them all.

But anon the great San Philip, she bethought herself and went
Having that within her womb that had left her ill content;
And the rest they came aboard us, and they fought us hand to hand,
For a dozen times they came with their pikes and musketeers,
And a dozen times we shook 'em off as a dog that shakes his ears
When he leaps from the water to the land.

And the sun went down, and the stars came out far over the summer
   sea,
But never a moment ceased the fight of the one and the fifty-three.
Ship after ship, the whole night long, their high-built galleons came,
Ship after ship, the whole night long, with her battle-thunder and flame;
Ship after ship, the whole night long, drew back with her dead and
   her shame.
For some were sunk and many were shattered, and so could fight us
   no more –
God of battles, was ever a battle like this in the world before?

For he said 'Fight on! fight on!'
Though his vessel was all but a wreck;
And it chanced, that when half of the short summer night was gone,
With a grisly wound to be dressed he had left the deck,
But a bullet struck him that was dressing it suddenly dead,
And himself he was wounded again in the side and the head,
And he said 'Fight on! fight on!'

And the night went down, and the sun smiled out far over the
    summer sea,
And the Spanish fleet with broken sides lay round us all in a ring;
But they dared not touch us again, for they feared that we still could
    sting,
So they watched what the end would be.
And we had not fought them in vain,
But in perilous plight were we,
Seeing forty of our poor hundred were slain,
And half of the rest of us maimed for life
In the crash of the cannonades and the desperate strife;
And the sick men down in the hold were most of them stark and cold,
And the pikes were all broken or bent, and the powder was all of it
    spent;
And the masts and the rigging were lying over the side;
But Sir Richard cried in his English pride,
'We have fought such a fight for a day and a night
As may never be fought again!
We have won great glory, my men!
And a day less or more,
At sea or ashore,
We die – does it matter when?
Sink me the ship, Master Gunner, sink her, split her in twain!
Fall into the hands of God, not into the hands of Spain!'

And the gunner said 'Ay, ay,' but the seamen made reply:
'We have children, we have wives,
And the Lord hath spared our lives.
We will make the Spaniard promise, if we yield, to let us go;
We shall live to fight again and to strike another blow.'
And the lion there lay dying, and they yielded to the foe.

And the stately Spanish men to their flagship bore him then,
Where they laid him by the mast, old Sir Richard caught at last,
And they praised him to his face with their courtly foreign grace;
But he rose upon their decks and he cried:
'I have fought for Queen and Faith like a valiant man and true;
I have only done my duty as a man is bound to do:
With a joyful spirit I Sir Richard Grenville die!'
And he fell upon their decks, and he died.

And they stared at the dead that had been so valiant and true,
And had holden the power and glory of Spain so cheap
That he dared her with one little ship and his English few;
Was he devil or man? He was devil for aught they knew,
But they sank his body with honour down into the deep,
And they manned the Revenge with a swarthier, alien crew,
And away she sailed with her loss and longed for her own;
When a wind from the lands they had ruined awoke from sleep,
And the water began to heave and the weather to moan,
And or ever that evening ended a great gale blew,
And a wave like the wave that is raised by an earthquake grew,
Till it smote on their hulls and their sails and their masts and their
    flags,
And the whole sea plunged and fell on the shot-shattered navy of
    Spain,
And the little Revenge herself went down by the island crags
To be lost evermore in the main.

ALFRED, LORD TENNYSON

The Old Navy

The captain stood on the carronade: 'First lieutenant,' says he,
'Send all my merry men aft here, for they must list to me;
I haven't the gift of the gab, my sons — because I'm bred to the sea;
That ship there is a Frenchman, who means to fight with we.
   And odds bobs, hammer and tongs, long as I've been to sea,
   I've fought 'gainst every odds — but I've gain'd the victory!

'That ship there is a Frenchman, and if we don't take she,
'Tis a thousand bullets to one, that she will capture we;
I haven't the gift of the gab, my boys; so each man to his gun;
If she's not mine in half an hour, I'll flog each mother's son.
   For odds bobs, hammer and tongs, long as I've been to sea,
   I've fought 'gainst every odds — and I've gain'd the victory!

We fought for twenty minutes, when the Frenchman had enough;
'I little thought,' said he, 'that your men were of such stuff';
Our captain took the Frenchman's sword, a low bow made to he;
'I haven't the gift of the gab, monsieur, but polite I wish to be.
   And odds bobs, hammer and tongs, long as I've been to sea,
   I've fought 'gainst every odds — and I've gain'd the victory!

Our captain sent for all of us: 'My merry men,' said he,
'I haven't the gift of the gab, my lads, but yet I thankful be:
You've done your duty handsomely, each man stood to his gun;
If you hadn't, you villains, as sure as day, I'd have flogg'd each
     mother's son,
   For odds bobs, hammer and tongs, as long as I'm at sea,
   I'll fight 'gainst every odds — and I'll gain the victory!

FREDERICK MARRYAT

Song of the Galley-slaves

We pulled for you when the wind was against us and the sails were
low.

Will you never let us go?

We ate bread and onions when you took towns, or ran aboard
quickly when you were beaten back by the foe.

The captains walked up and down the deck in fair weather singing
songs, but we were below.

We fainted with our chins on the oars and you did not see that they
were idle, for we still swung to and fro.

Will you never let us go?

The salt made our oar-handles like shark-skin; our knees were cut to
the bone with salt-cracks; our hair was stuck to our foreheads; and
our lips were cut to the gums, and you whipped us because we
could not row.

Will you never let us go?

But, in a little time, we shall run out of the port-holes as the water
runs along the oar-blade, and though you tell the others to row
after us you will never catch us till you catch the oar-thresh and
tie up the winds in the belly of the sail. Aho!

Will you never let us go?

RUDYARD KIPLING

Boots

We're foot— slog— slog— slog— sloggin' over Africa —
Foot— slog— slog— slog— sloggin' over Africa —
(Boots — boots — boots — boots — movin' up and down again!)
　　There's no discharge in the war!

Seven — six — eleven — five — nine-an'-twenty mile today —
Four — eleven — seventeen — thirty-two the day before —
(Boots — boots — boots — boots — movin' up and down again!)
　　There's no discharge in the war!

Don't — don't — don't — don't — look at what's in front of you.
(Boots — boots — boots — boots — movin' up an' down again);
Men — men — men — men — men go mad with watchin' em,
　　An' there's no discharge in the war!

Try — try — try — try — to think o' something different —
Oh — my — God — keep — me from goin' lunatic!
(Boots — boots — boots — boots — movin' up an' down again!)
　　There's no discharge in the war!

Count – count – count – count – the bullets in the bandoliers.
If – your – eyes – drop – they will get atop of you!
(Boots – boots – boots – boots – movin' up and down again)
    There's no discharge in the war!

We – can – stick – out – 'unger, thirst, an' weariness,
But – not – not – not – not the chronic sight of 'em –
Boots – boots – boots – boots – movin' up an' down again,
    An' there's no discharge in the war!

'Tain't – so – bad – by – day because o' company,
But night – brings – long – strings – o' forty thousand million
Boots – boots – boots – boots – movin' up an' down again.
    There's no discharge in the war!

I – 'ave – marched – six – weeks in 'Ell an' certify
It – is – not – fire – devils – dark or anything,
But boots – boots – boots – boots – movin' up an' down again,
    An' there's no discharge in the war!

RUDYARD KIPLING

RIDDLES AND PUNS
AND
RUM CONUNDRUMS

Who, Sir, am I?

Who, sir, am I?
For a start, I hate sunshine
And deserve the penalty –
To be swallowed with good wine.
Miserable slitherer,
Landlubberly crustacean;
The French eat me, sir.
They are a wise nation!

JOHN MOLE

snail

I am the Shame beneath a Carpet

I am the shame beneath a carpet.
No one comes to sweep me off my feet.

Abandoned rooms and unread books collect me.
Sometimes I dance like particles of light.

My legions thicken on each window pane,
A gathering of dusk, perpetual gloom,

And when at last the house has fallen,
I am the cloud left hanging in the air.

JOHN MOLE

dust

Humpty Dumpty's Poem

(from *Through the Looking-Glass*)

In winter, when the fields are white,
I sing this song for your delight –
*   *   *

In spring, when woods are getting green,
I'll try and tell you what I mean.
*   *   *

In summer, when the days are long,
Perhaps you'll understand the song:

In autumn, when the leaves are brown,
Take pen and ink, and write it down.
*   *   *

I sent a message to the fish:
I told them 'This is what I wish.'

The little fishes of the sea,
They sent an answer back to me.

The little fishes' answer was
'We cannot do it, Sir, because –'
*   *   *

I sent to them again to say
'It will be better to obey.'

The fishes answered with a grin,
'Why, what a temper you are in!'

I told them once, I told them twice:
They would not listen to advice.

I took a kettle large and new,
Fit for the deed I had to do.

My heart went hop, my heart went thump:
I filled the kettle at the pump.

Then someone came to me and said,
'The little fishes are in bed.'

I said to him, I said it plain,
'Then you must wake them up again.'

I said it very loud and clear;
I went and shouted in his ear.

*   *   *

But he was very stiff and proud;
He said 'You needn't shout so loud!'

And he was very proud and stiff;
He said 'I'd go and wake them, if —'

I took a corkscrew from the shelf;
I went to wake them up myself.

And when I found the door was locked,
I pulled and pushed and kicked and knocked.

And when I found the door was shut,
I tried to turn the handle, but —

LEWIS CARROLL

They Told Me
You Had Been to Her

(from *Alice in Wonderland*)

They told me you had been to her,
 And mentioned me to him:
She gave me a good character,
 But said I could not swim.

He sent them word I had not gone
 (We know it to be true):
If she should push the matter on,
 What would become of you?

I gave her one, they gave him two,
    You gave us three or more;
They all returned from him to you,
    Though they were mine before.

If I or she should chance to be
    Involved in this affair,
He trusts to you to set them free,
    Exactly as we were.

My notion was that you had been
    (Before she had this fit)
An obstacle that came between
    Him, and ourselves, and it.

Don't let him know she liked them best,
    For this must ever be
A secret, kept from all the rest,
    Between yourself and me.

LEWIS CARROLL

You Tell Me

Here are the football results:
League Division Fun
Manchester United won, Manchester City lost.
Crystal Palace 2, Buckingham Palace 1
Millwall Leeds nowhere
Wolves 8 A cheese roll and had a cup of tea 2
Aldershot 3 Buffalo Bill shot 2
Evertonill, Liverpool's not very well either
Newcastle's Heaven Sunderland's a very nice place 2
Ipswhich one? You tell me.

MICHAEL ROSEN

AWFUL
WARNINGS

Henry King

Who chewed bits of String, and was early cut off in Dreadful Agonies.

The Chief Defect of Henry King
    Was chewing little bits of String.
At last he swallowed some which tied
    Itself in ugly Knots inside.
Physicians of the Utmost Fame
Were called at once; but when they came
They answered, as they took their Fees,
'There is no Cure for this Disease.
Henry will very soon be dead.'
His Parents stood about his Bed
Lamenting his Untimely Death,
When Henry, with his Latest Breath,
Cried – 'Oh, my Friends, be warned by me,
That Breakfast, Dinner, Lunch, and Tea
Are all the Human Frame requires ...'
With that, the Wretched Child expires.

HILAIRE BELLOC

George

Who played with a Dangerous Toy, and suffered a Catastrophe of considerable Dimensions.

When George's Grandmamma was told
That George had been as good as Gold,
She Promised in the Afternoon
To buy him an *Immense BALLOON*.

And so she did; but when it came,
It got into the candle flame,
And being of a dangerous sort
Exploded with a loud report!

The Lights went out! The Windows broke!
The Room was filled with reeking smoke.
And in the darkness shrieks and yells
Were mingled with Electric Bells,
And falling masonry and groans,
And crunching, as of broken bones,
And dreadful shrieks, when, worst of all,
The House itself began to fall!
It tottered, shuddering to and fro,
Then crashed into the street below –
Which happened to be Savile Row.

When Help arrived, among the Dead
Were Cousin Mary, Little Fred,
The Footmen (both of them), the Groom,
The man that cleaned the Billiard-Room,
The Chaplain, and the Still-Room Maid.
And I am dreadfully afraid
That Monsieur Champignon, the Chef,
Will now be permanently deaf —
And both his Aides are much the same;
While George, who was in part to blame,
Received, you will regret to hear,
A nasty lump behind the ear.

Moral

The moral is that little Boys
Should not be given dangerous Toys.

HILAIRE BELLOC

A Cautionary Tale

Every addled egg
A birdsnester blows
Is one more blood-knot
Severed.
        Plenty
Were blown, and plenty dropped
From the treetops
In Wayland Wood last spring
By butterfingered boys.
             Then
One of the birdsnesters slipped
And fell, a boy named Jones
The papers said,
Top-heavy, head-first,
His feet the flight
Of an arrow whose head
Was his.
       Slipped, fell –
And his young yolk spilled
From its fragile shell
High in the leafless
Tree of himself; and Jones
Was a lifeless
Bundle of bones
And puddle of bloody shadow.
There are fewer
Boys, there are far more
Birds, in Wayland Wood
This spring.

NIGEL LEWIS

Dane-geld

It is always a temptation to an armed and agile nation
  To call upon a neighbour and to say:
'We invaded you last night – we are quite prepared to fight,
  Unless you pay us cash to go away.'

    And that is called asking for Dane-geld,
      And the people who ask it explain
    That you've only to pay 'em the Dane-geld
      And then you'll get rid of the Dane!

It is always a temptation to a rich and lazy nation,
  To puff and look important and to say:
'Though we know we should defeat you, we have not the time to
    meet you.
  We will therefore pay you cash to go away.'

    And that is called paying the Dane-geld;
      But we've proved it again and again,
    That if once you have paid him the Dane-geld
      You never get rid of the Dane.

It is wrong to put temptation in the path of any nation,
  For fear they should succumb and go astray;
So when you are requested to pay up or be molested,
  You will find it better policy to say:

    'We never pay *any*one Dane-geld,
      No matter how trifling the cost;
    For the end of that game is oppression and shame,
      And the nation that plays it is lost!'

RUDYARD KIPLING

The Huntsman

Kagwa hunted the lion,
  Through bush and forest went his spear.
One day he found the skull of a man
  And said to it, 'How did you come here?'
The skull opened its mouth and said,
  'Talking brought me here.'

Kagwa hurried home;
    Went to the king's chair and spoke:
'In the forest I found a talking skull.'
    The king was silent. Then he said slowly,
'Never since I was born of my mother
    Have I seen or heard of a skull which spoke.'

The king called out to his guards:
    'Two of you now go with him
And find this talking skull;
    But if his tale is a lie
And the skull speaks no word,
    This Kagwa himself must die.'

They rode into the forest;
    For days and nights they found nothing.
At last they saw the skull; Kagwa
    Said to it, 'How did you come here?'
The skull said nothing. Kagwa implored,
    But the skull said nothing.

The guards said, 'Kneel down.'
    They killed him with sword and spear.
Then the skull opened its mouth;
    'Huntsman, how did you come here?'
And the dead man answered,
    'Talking brought me here.'

EDWARD LOWBURY

The Inchcape Rock

No stir in the air, no stir in the sea,
The ship was as still as she could be,
Her sails from heaven received no motion,
Her keel was steady in the ocean.

Without either sign or sound of their shock
The waves flow'd o'er the Inchcape Rock;
So little they rose, so little they fell,
They did not move the Inchcape Bell.

The good old Abbot of Aberbrothok
Had placed that bell on the Inchcape Rock;
On a buoy in the storm it floated and swung,
And over the waves its warning rung.

When the rock was hid by the surges' swell,
The mariners heard the warning bell;
And then they knew the perilous Rock,
And blessed the Abbot of Aberbrothok.

The sun in heaven was shining gay,
All things were joyful on that day;
The sea-birds screamed as they wheeled round,
And there was joyance in their sound.

The buoy of the Inchcape Bell was seen
A darker speck on the ocean green;
Sir Ralph the Rover walked his deck,
And he fixed his eye on the darker speck.

He felt the cheering power of spring,
It made him whistle, it made him sing;
His heart was mirthful to excess,
But the Rover's mirth was wickedness.

His eye was on the Inchcape float;
Quoth he, 'My men, put out the boat,
And row me to the Inchcape Rock,
And I'll plague the priest of Aberbrothok.'

The boat is lowered, the boatmen row,
And to the Inchcape Rock they go;
Sir Ralph bent over from the boat
And he cut the bell of the Inchcape float.

Down sank the bell, with a gurgling sound,
The bubbles rose and burst around;
Quoth Sir Ralph, 'The next who comes to the Rock
Won't bless the Abbot of Aberbrothok.'

Sir Ralph the Rover sailed away,
He scoured the seas for many a day;
And now grown rich with plundered store,
He steers his course for Scotland's shore.

So thick a haze o'erspreads the sky
They cannot see the sun on high;
The wind hath blown a gale all day,
At evening it hath died away.

On the deck the Rover takes his stand,
So dark it is they see no land.
Quoth Sir Ralph, 'It will be lighter soon,
For there is the dawn of the rising moon.'

'Canst hear,' said one, 'the breakers roar?
For methinks we should be near the shore;
Now where we are I cannot tell,
But I wish I could hear the Inchcape Bell.'

They hear no sound, the swell is strong;
Though the wind hath fallen, they drift along,
Till the vessel strikes with a shivering shock;
Cried they, 'It is the Inchcape Rock!'

Sir Ralph the Rover tore his hair,
He cursed himself in his despair;
The waves rush in on every side,
The ship is sinking beneath the tide,

But even in his dying fear
One dreadful sound could the Rover hear,
A sound as if with the Inchcape Bell,
The fiends below were ringing his knell.

ROBERT SOUTHEY

The Lion and Albert

There's a famous seaside place called Blackpool,
    That's noted for fresh air and fun,
And Mr and Mrs Ramsbottom
    Went there with young Albert, their son.

A grand little lad was young Albert,
    All dressed in his best; quite a swell
With a stick with an 'orse's 'ead 'andle,
    The finest that Woolworth's could sell.

They didn't think much to the Ocean:
    The waves, they was fiddlin' and small,
There was no wrecks and nobody drownded,
    Fact, nothing to laugh at at all.

So, seeking for further amusement,
    They paid and went into the Zoo,
Where they'd Lions and Tigers and Camels,
    And old ale and sandwiches too.

There were one great big Lion called Wallace;
    His nose were all covered with scars –
He lay in a somnolent posture
    With the side of his face on the bars.

Now Albert had heard about Lions,
    How they was ferocious and wild –
To see Wallace lying so peaceful,
    Well, it didn't seem right to the child.

So straightway the brave little feller,
    Not showing a morsel of fear,
Took his stick with its 'orse's 'ead 'andle
    And poked it in Wallace's ear.

You could see that the Lion didn't like it,
    For giving a kind of a roll,
He pulled Albert inside the cage with 'im,
    And swallowed the little lad 'ole.

Then Pa, who had seen the occurrence,
    And didn't know what to do next,
Said 'Mother! Yon Lion's 'et Albert,'
    And Mother said 'Well, I am vexed!'

Then Mr and Mrs Ramsbottom —
    Quite rightly, when all's said and done —
Complained to the Animal Keeper
    That the Lion had eaten their son.

The keeper was quite nice about it;
    He said 'What a nasty mishap.
Are you sure that it's *your* boy he's eaten?'
    Pa said 'Am I sure? There's his cap!'

The manager had to be sent for.
    He came and he said 'What's to do?'
Pa said 'Yon Lion's 'et Albert,
    And 'im in his Sunday clothes, too.'

Then Mother said, 'Right's right, young feller;
   I think it's a shame and a sin
For a lion to go and eat Albert,
   And after we've paid to come in.'

The manager wanted no trouble,
   He took out his purse right away,
Saying 'How much to settle the matter?'
   And Pa said 'What do you usually pay?'

But Mother had turned a bit awkward
   When she thought where her Albert had gone.
She said 'No! someone's got to be summonsed' –
   So that was decided upon.

Then off they went to the P'lice Station,
   In front of the Magistrate chap;
They told 'im what happened to Albert,
   And proved it by showing his cap.

The Magistrate gave his opinion
   That no one was really to blame
And he said that he hoped the Ramsbottoms
   Would have further sons to their name.

At that Mother got proper blazing,
   'And thank you, sir, kindly,' said she.
'What, waste all our lives raising children
   To feed ruddy Lions? Not me!'

MARRIOTT EDGAR

Pride

Two birds sat in a Big White Bra
   That swung as it hung
   On the washing-line.

They sang: 'Hurray!' and they sang: 'Hurrah!
Of all the birds we're the best by far!
Our hammock swings to the highest star!
   No life like yours and mine!'

They were overheard
   By a third
   Bird

That swooped down on to a nearby tree
And sneered: 'Knickers! It's plain to see
A bird in a tree is worth two in a bra.
   There's no bird *half* so fine!'

And it seemed indeed that he was right
For the washing-line was *far* too tight
And old and frayed. As the laundry flapped,
The big wind heaved and the rope ... *snapped!*

You should have heard
   The third
   Bird.

He cried: 'Aha!
For all their chatter and la-de-dah,
They didn't get far in their Big White Bra!
If there *is* a bird who's a Superstar,
It's me, it's me, it's me!'

Down to the ground
He dived in his glee

And the Big Black Cat
Enjoyed his tea.

KIT WRIGHT

Bad Sir Brian Botany

Sir Brian had a battleaxe with great big knobs on;
    He went among the villagers and blipped them on the head.
On Wednesday and on Saturday, but mostly on the latter day,
    He called at all the cottages, and this is what he said:
        'I am Sir Brian!' (*ting-ling*)
         'I am Sir Brian!' (*rat-tat*)
       'I am Sir Brian, as bold as a lion –
         Take *that!* – and *that!* – and *that!*'

Sir Brian had a pair of boots with great big spurs on,
    A fighting pair of which he was particularly fond.
On Tuesday and on Friday, just to make the street look tidy,
    He'd collect the passing villagers and kick them in the pond.
        'I am Sir Brian!' (*sper-lash!*)
         'I am Sir Brian!' (*sper-losh!*)
       'I am Sir Brian, as bold as a lion –
         Is anyone else for a wash?'

Sir Brian woke one morning, and he couldn't find his battleaxe;
    He walked into the village in his second pair of boots.
He had gone a hundred paces, when the street was full of faces,
    And the villagers were round him with ironical salutes.
        'You are Sir Brian? Indeed!
         You are Sir Brian? Dear, dear!
       You are Sir Brian, as bold as a lion?
         Delighted to meet you here!'

Sir Brian went a journey, and he found a lot of duckweed:
  They pulled him out and dried him, and they blipped him on the
    head.
They took him by the breeches, and they hurled him into ditches,
  And they pushed him under waterfalls, and this is what they said:
    'You are Sir Brian – don't laugh,
      You are Sir Brian – don't cry;
    You are Sir Brian, as bold as a lion –
      Sir Brian, the lion, good-bye!'

Sir Brian struggled home again, and chopped up his battleaxe,
  Sir Brian took his fighting boots, and threw them in the fire.
He is quite a different person now he hasn't got his spurs on,
  And he goes about the village as B. Botany, Esquire.
    'I am Sir Brian? Oh, *no!*
      I am Sir Brian? Who's he?
    I haven't got any title, I'm Botany –
      Plain Mr Botany (B).'

A. A. MILNE

The New Vestments

There lived an old man in the Kingdom of Tess,
Who invented a purely original dress;
And when it was perfectly made and complete,
He opened the door, and walked into the street.

By way of a hat, he'd a loaf of Brown Bread,
In the middle of which he inserted his head —
His Shirt was made up of no end of dead Mice,
The warmth of whose skins was quite fluffy and nice —
His Drawers were of Rabbit-skins — so were his Shoes —
His Stockings were skins — but it is not known whose —
His Waistcoat and Trousers were made of Pork Chops —
His Buttons were Jujubes, and Chocolate Drops —
His Coat was all Pancakes with Jam for a border,
And a girdle of Biscuits to keep it in order;
And he wore over all, as a screen from bad weather,
A Cloak of green Cabbage-leaves stitched all together.

He had walked a short way, when he heard a great noise,
Of all sorts of Beasticles, Birdlings, and Boys —
And from every long street and dark lane in the town
Beasts, Birdles, and Boys in a tumult rushed down.
Two Cows and a half ate his Cabbage-leaf Cloak —
Four Apes seized his Girdle, which vanished like smoke —
Three Kids ate up half of his Pancaky Coat —
And the tails were devour'd by an ancient He Goat —
An army of Dogs in a twinkling tore *up* his
Pork Waistcoat and Trousers to give to their Puppies —

And while they were growling, and mumbling the Chops,
Ten Boys prigged the Jujubes and Chocolate Drops –
He tried to run back to his house, but in vain,
For Scores of fat Pigs came again and again –
They rushed out of stables and hovels and doors –
They tore off his stockings, his shoes, and his drawers –
And now from the housetops with screechings descend,
Striped, spotted, white, black, and gray Cats without end,
They jumped on his shoulders and knocked off his hat –
When Crows, Ducks, and Hens made a mincemeat of that –
They speedily flew at his sleeves in a trice,
And utterly tore up his Shirt of dead Mice –
They swallowed the last of his Shirt with a squall –
Whereon he ran home with no clothes on at all.

And he said to himself as he bolted the door,
'I will not wear a similar dress any more,
'Any more, any more, any more, never more!'

EDWARD LEAR

SONGS AND
SILENCES

The Wraggle Taggle Gypsies

Three gypsies stood at the Castle gate,
　　They sang so high, they sang so low,
The lady sate in her chamber late,
　　Her heart it melted away as snow.

They sang so sweet, they sang so shrill,
　　That fast her tears began to flow.
And she laid down her silken gown,
　　Her golden rings and all her show.

She plucked off her high-heeled shoes,
　　A-made of Spanish leather, O!
She would in the street, with her bare, bare feet,
　　All out in the wind and weather, O!

It was late last night, when my lord came home,
　　Enquiring for his a-lady, O!
The servants said on every hand,
　　'She's gone with the wraggle taggle gypsies, O!'

'O saddle to me my milk-white steed.
   Go and fetch me my pony, O!
That I may ride and seek my bride,
   Who is gone with the wraggle taggle gypsies, O!'

O he rode high and he rode low,
   He rode through woods and copses too,
Until he came to an open field,
   And there he espied his a-lady, O!

'What makes you leave your house and land?
   What makes you leave your money, O?
What makes you leave your new-wedded lord,
   To go with the wraggle taggle gypsies, O?'

'What care I for my house and my land?
   What care I for my money, O?
What care I for my new-wedded lord?
   I'm off with the wraggle taggle gypsies, O!'

'Last night you slept on a goose-feather bed,
   With the sheet turned down so bravely, O!
And to-night you'll sleep in a cold open field,
   Along with the wraggle taggle gypsies, O!'

'What care I for a goose-feather bed,
   With the sheet turned down so bravely, O?
For to-night I shall sleep in a cold open field,
   Along with the wraggle taggle gypsies, O!'

                                        ANON.

Lord of the Dance

I danced in the morning
When the world was begun,
And I danced in the moon
And the stars and the sun
And I came down from heaven
And I danced on the earth –
At Bethlehem I had my birth.

Dance then wherever you may be;
I am the Lord of the Dance, said he,
I'll lead you all, wherever you may be,
I will lead you all in the Dance, said he.

I danced for the scribe
And the pharisee,
But they would not dance
And they couldn't follow me;
I danced for the fishermen,
For James and John –
They came with me
And the dance went on.

I danced on the Sabbath
And I cured the lame;
The holy people
Said it was a shame;
They whipped and they stripped
And they hung me high,
And they left me there
On a Cross to die.

I danced on a Friday
When the sky turned black –
It's hard to dance
With the devil on your back;
They buried my body
And they thought I'd gone –
But I am the dance
And I still go on.

They cut me down
And I leapt up high –
I am the life
That'll never, never die;
I'll live in you
If you'll live in me –
I am the Lord
Of the Dance, said he.

Dance then wherever you may be;
I am the Lord of the Dance, said he,
I'll lead you all, wherever you may be,
I will lead you all in the Dance, said he.

SYDNEY CARTER

The Song of Wandering Aengus

I went out to the hazel wood,
Because a fire was in my head,
And cut and peeled a hazel wand,
And hooked a berry to a thread;
And when white moths were on the wing,
And moth-like stars were flickering out,
I dropped the berry in a stream
And caught a little silver trout.

When I had laid it on the floor
I went to blow the fire a-flame,
But something rustled on the floor,
And someone called me by my name:
It had become a glimmering girl
With apple blossom in her hair
Who called me by my name and ran
And faded through the brightening air.

Though I am old with wandering
Through hollow lands and hilly lands,
I will find out where she has gone,
And kiss her lips and take her hands;
And walk among long dappled grass,
And pluck till time and times are done
The silver apples of the moon,
The golden apples of the sun.

W. B. YEATS

Rolling Down to Rio

I've never sailed the Amazon,
   I've never reached Brazil;
But the *Don* and *Magdalena*,
   They can go there when they will!

            Yes, weekly from Southampton,
            Great steamers, white and gold,
            Go rolling down to Rio
            (Roll down – roll down to Rio!)
            And I'd like to roll to Rio
            Some day before I'm old!

I've never seen a Jaguar,
   Nor yet an Armadill-
o dilloing in his armour,
   And I s'pose I never will,

            Unless I go to Rio
            These wonders to behold –
            Roll down – roll down to Rio –
            Roll really down to Rio!
            Oh, I'd love to roll to Rio
            Some day before I'm old!

RUDYARD KIPLING

Eldorado

Gaily bedight,
A gallant knight,
In sunshine and in shadow,
Had journeyed long,
Singing a song,
In search of Eldorado.

But he grew old –
This knight so bold –
And o'er his heart a shadow
Fell as he found
No spot of ground
That looked like Eldorado.

And, as his strength
Failed him at length,
He met a pilgrim shadow;
'Shadow,' said he,
'Where can it be,
This land of Eldorado?'

'Over the mountains
Of the Moon,
Down the valley of the Shadow,
Ride, boldly ride,'
The shade replied,
'If you seek for Eldorado.'

EDGAR ALLAN POE

Barrel Organ Song

I'm a Czechoslovakian drowned sailor-man,
My name is Frantishek,
When I was alive, I whistled this song
As I swabbed the lower deck:

O happy was I, happy was I, happy as can be,
With a maiden called Euphoria, sitting on my knee.

Now I live with a mermaid beneath the waves,
A girl salty and sweet.
I'm her only dear darling of all the drowned
Czechoslovakian fleet.

O happy am I, happy am I, happy as can be,
With a maiden called Euphoria, sitting on my knee.

GERDA MAYER

The Sands of Dee

'O Mary, go and call the cattle home,
    And call the cattle home,
    And call the cattle home
  Across the sands of Dee';
The western wind was wild and dank with foam,
  And all alone went she.
The western tide crept up along the sand,
    And o'er and o'er the sand,
    And round and round the sand,
  As far as eye could see.
The rolling mist came down and hid the land:
  And never home came she.

'Oh! is it weed, or fish, or floating hair –
    A tress of golden hair,
    A drownèd maiden's hair
  Above the nets at sea?
Was never salmon yet that shone so fair
  Among the stakes on Dee.'

They rowed her in across the rolling foam,
    The cruel crawling foam,
    The cruel hungry foam,
  To her grave beside the sea:
But still the boatmen hear her call the cattle home
    Across the sands of Dee.

CHARLES KINGSLEY

Slow Guitar

(from *Didn't He Ramble*)

Bring me now where the warm wind
blows, where the grasses
sigh, where the sweet
tongued blossom flowers

where the showers
fan soft like a fisherman's
net through the sweet-
ened air

Bring me now where the workers
rest, where the cotton drifts,
where the rivers are
and the minstrel sits

on the logwood stump
with the dreams of his slow guitar.

EDWARD BRATHWAITE

A Piper

A piper in the streets today
Set up and tuned and started to play
And away, away, away on the tide
Of his music he started. On every side
Doors and windows were opened wide,
And men left down their work and came,
And women with petticoats coloured like flame,
And little bare feet that were blue with cold
Went dancing back to the age of gold,
And all the world went gay, went gay
For half an hour in the street today.

SEUMAS O'SULLIVAN

Where the Bee Sucks

Where the bee sucks, there suck I,
In a cowslip's bell I lie,
There I couch when owls do cry;
On the bat's back I do fly
After summer merrily.
Merrily, merrily, shall I live now
Under the blossom that hangs on the bough.

WILLIAM SHAKESPEARE

Under the Greenwood Tree

Under the greenwood tree,
Who loves to lie with me,
And turn his merry note
Unto the sweet bird's throat:
Come hither, come hither, come hither,
    Here shall he see no enemy
But winter and rough weather.

Who doth ambition shun
And loves to live i' the sun,
Seeking the food he eats
And pleased with what he gets:
Come hither, come hither, come hither,
    Here shall he see no enemy
But winter and rough weather.

WILLIAM SHAKESPEARE

Sing Me a Song

Sing me a song of a lad that is gone,
    Say, could that lad be I?
Merry of soul he sailed on a day
    Over the sea to Skye.

Mull was astern, Rum on the port,
    Eigg on the starboard bow;
Glory of youth glowed in his soul:
    Where is that glory now?

Sing me a song of a lad that is gone,
    Say, could that lad be I?
Merry of soul he sailed on a day
    Over the sea to Skye.

Give me again all that was here,
    Give me the sun that shone!
Give me the eyes, give me the soul,
    Give me the lad that's gone!

Sing me a song of a lad that is gone,
    Say, could that lad be I?
Merry of soul he sailed on a day
    Over the sea to Skye.

Billows and breeze, islands and seas,
    Mountains of rain and sun,
All that was good, all that was fair,
    All that was me is gone.

ROBERT LOUIS STEVENSON

Song

When I am dead, my dearest,
    Sing no sad songs for me;
Plant thou no roses at my head,
    Nor shady cypress tree:
Be the green grass above me
    With showers and dewdrops wet;
And if thou wilt, remember,
    And if thou wilt, forget.

I shall not see the shadows,
    I shall not feel the rain;
I shall not hear the nightingale
    Sing on, as if in pain;
And dreaming through the twilight
    That doth nor rise nor set,
Haply I may remember,
    And haply may forget.

CHRISTINA ROSSETTI

Skipping Rhyme

Páin óf the léaf óne twó –
Wórd óf the stóne, thrée, fóur –
Fóot óf the dárk, pít óf the hánd,
Heárt óf the clóud, fíve, síx, and
Oút!
    Skíp.
Nóra she had whíte eýes,
Máry she had bláck –
Hélen loóked in Gréy Man's Wóod and
Néver came
Báck!
    Jump.
Nóra dráws a gréen threád,
Máry spíns it blúe –
But Hélen wíll not bínd it tíll her
Trúe Love mákes it
Trúe!
    Quíck!
Óne, twó, leáf of the páin,
Thrée, foúr, stóne of the wórd,
Fíve, síx, dárk of the fóot, hánd of the pít,
Clóud of the heárt, and
OÚT!

ALAN BROWNJOHN

Lauds

Among the leaves the small birds sing;
The crow of the cock commands awaking:
In solitude, for company.

Bright shines the sun on creatures mortal;
Men of their neighbours become sensible:
In solitude, for company.

The crow of the cock commands awaking;
Already the mass-bell goes dong-ding:
In solitude, for company.

Men of their neighbours become sensible;
God bless the Realm, God bless the People:
In solitude, for company.

Already the mass-bell goes dong-ding:
The dripping mill-wheel is again turning:
In solitude, for company.

God bless the Realm, God bless the People;
God bless this green world temporal:
In solitude, for company.

The dripping mill-wheel is again turning;
Among the leaves the small birds sing:
In solitude, for company.

W. H. AUDEN

Index of First Lines

Index of Poets

Acknowledgements

The editor and publishers gratefully acknowledge permission to reproduce copyright poems in this book.

'Lauds' by W. H. Auden from *Collected Poems*, reprinted by permission of Faber and Faber Ltd and Random House, New York; 'Worm Sonnet' by Michael Baldwin from *The Old Gnat's Daughter*, reprinted by permission of the author; 'Tom and His Pony, Jack', 'Jack and His Pony, Tom', 'Lord Hippo', 'George' and 'Henry King' by Hilaire Belloc from *The Complete Verse*, reprinted by permission of Gerald Duckworth & Co. Ltd; 'Hunter Trials' by John Betjeman from *Collected Poems*, reprinted by permission of John Murray (Publishers) Ltd; 'Slow Guitar' by Edward Brathwaite, © Oxford University Press 1967. Reprinted from *Rights of Passage* by Edward Brathwaite (1967) by permission of Oxford University Press; 'Skipping Rhyme' and 'After Prévert' by Alan Brownjohn from *Collected Poems 1952–1983*, reprinted by permission of the author and Secker & Warburg Ltd; 'Lord of the Dance' by Sydney Carter, reprinted by permission of the author and of Stainer & Bell Ltd; 'Nursery Rhyme of Innocence and Experience' by Charles Causley from *Collected Poems 1951–1975* and 'Colonel Fazackerley' by Charles Causley from *Figgie Hobbin*, reprinted by permission of the author and Macmillan Ltd; 'The Lost Heifer' by Austin Clarke, reprinted by permission of the Dolmen Press Ltd; 'Sheep' by W. H. Davies from *The Complete Poems of W. H. Davies*, reprinted by permission of the Executors of the W. H. Davies Estate and Jonathan Cape Ltd; 'The Listeners' by Walter de la Mare, reprinted by permission of the Trustees of Walter de la Mare and the Society of Authors as their representative; 'Alternative Endings to an Unwritten Ballad' by Paul Dehn, Copyright © 1965, 1976 Dehn Enterprises Ltd, used with permission from Hamish Hamilton Ltd; 'The Lion and Albert' by Marriott Edgar, reprinted by permission of International Music Publications; 'A Book of Ghosts' by Philip Ennis, reprinted by permission of the author; 'When I Was Your Age' by Michael Frayn from *Allsorts 7*, reprinted by permission of Methuen Children's Books; 'Stopping by Woods on a Snowy Evening' by Robert Frost from *The Poetry of Robert Frost*, edited by Edward Connery Latham, reprinted by permission of the Estate of Robert Frost, the editor and Jonathan Cape Ltd; 'Flannan Isle' by Wilfrid Gibson from *Collected Poems*, reprinted by permission of Mr

Michael Gibson and Macmillan, London and Basingstoke; 'The Door' by Miroslav Holub from *Selected Poems* (Penguin Modern European Poets), reprinted by permission of Penguin Books Ltd; 'Loveliest of Trees' by A. E. Housman, reprinted by permission of the Society of Authors as the literary representative of the Estate of A. E. Housman, and Jonathan Cape Ltd, publishers of A. E. Housman's *Collected Poems*; 'My Father' by Ted Hughes, reprinted by permission of Faber and Faber Ltd from *Meet My Folks* by Ted Hughes; 'The Way through the Woods', 'A Smuggler's Song', 'Song of the Galley-slaves', 'Boots', 'Dane-geld', 'The Camel's Hump' and 'Rolling Down to Rio' by Rudyard Kipling, reprinted by permission of the National Trust for Places of Historic Interest or Natural Beauty and Macmillan, London, Ltd; 'Bat' by D. H. Lawrence from *The Complete Poems of D. H. Lawrence*, reprinted by permission of Laurence Pollinger Ltd and the Estate of Mrs Frieda Lawrence Ravagli; 'A Cautionary Tale' by Nigel Lewis, reprinted by permission of the author; 'The Flower-fed Buffaloes' by Vachel Lindsay from *Going-to-the-Stars*, copyright 1926 by D. Appleton & Co., renewed 1954 by Elizabeth Lindsay, reprinted by permission of E. P. Dutton & Co. Inc.; 'The Huntsman' by Edward Lowbury, reprinted by permission of the author; 'The Poem' from *The Complete Poetical Works* by Amy Lowell. Copyright © 1955 by Houghton Mifflin Company. Reprinted by permission of Houghton Mifflin Company; 'The Lesson' by Roger McGough from *In the Glassroom*, reprinted by permission of the author and Jonathan Cape Ltd; an extract from 'Reynard the Fox' by John Masefield, reprinted by permission of the Society of Authors as the literary representative of the Estate of John Masefield; 'Shallow Poem' and 'Barrel Organ Song' by Gerda Mayer, reprinted by permission of the author; 'Granny Boot' by Spike Milligan, reprinted by permission of the author: 'Bad Sir Brian Botany' by A. A. Milne from *When We Were Very Young*, reprinted by permission of Methuen Children's Books and McClelland & Stewart, Toronto; 'Who, Sir, am I?' and 'I am the Shame beneath a Carpet' by John Mole, reprinted by permission of the author; 'The Highwayman' by Alfred Noyes, reprinted by permission of Blackwood Pillans & Wilson Ltd; 'A Piper' by Seumas O'Sullivan, reprinted by permission of Mrs Frances Sommerville; 'The Ghoul' by Jack Prelutsky from *Nightmares*, Copyright © 1976 by Jack Prelutsky. Reprinted by permission of Greenwillow Books (a Division of William Morrow & Co.); 'The Old Wife and the Ghost' by James Reeves from *The Blackbird in the Lilac* by James Reeves (1952), reprinted by permission of Oxford University Press; 'You Tell Me' by Michael Rosen from *You Tell Me* by Roger McGough and Michael Rosen

(Viking Kestrel), reprinted by permission of Penguin Books Ltd; 'The Song of Tyrannosaurus Rex' by William Scammell, reprinted by permission of the author; 'Nettles', 'A Case of Murder' and 'The Lady and the Gypsy' by Vernon Scannell, reprinted by permission of the author; 'The Shooting of Dan McGrew' by Robert W. Service, reprinted by permission of the Estate of Robert W. Service; 'Tall Nettles' by Edward Thomas from *Collected Poems*, reprinted by permission of Faber and Faber Ltd and Myfanwy Thomas; 'Pride' by Kit Wright from *Hot Dog and Other Poems* (Viking Kestrel), reprinted by permission of Penguin Books Ltd; 'The Wild Swans at Coole' and 'The Song of Wandering Aengus' by W. B. Yeats from *The Collected Poems of W. B. Yeats*, reprinted by permission of Michael B. Yeats, Anne Yeats and Macmillan, London Ltd.

Every effort has been made to trace copyright holders but in a few cases this has proved impossible. The editor and publishers apologize for these unwilling cases of copyright transgression and would like to hear from any copyright holders not acknowledged.